CHILI

CRISP

CHILICRISPCHILIC
RISPCHILICRISPCH
CHILICRISPCHILIC
RISPCHILICRISPCH
CHILICRISPCHILIC
RISPCHILICRISPCH
CHILICRISPCHILIC
RISPCHILICRISPCH
CHILICRISPCHILIC
RISPCHILICRISPCH

CRISP CHILI CRISP CHI
ISP CHILI CRISP CHI
LI CRISP CHILI CRISP
ISP CHILI CRISP CHI
LI CRISP CHILI CRISP
ISP CHILI CRISP CHI
LI CRISP CHILI CRISP
ISP CHILI CRISP CHI
LI CRISP CHILI CRIS
ISP CHILI CRISP CHILI
LI CRISP CHILI CRIS
ISP CHILI CRISP CHILI
LI CRISP CHILI CRIS
ISP CHILI CRISP CHILI

50+
Recipes
to Satisfy
Your Spicy,
Crunchy,
Garlicky
Cravings

JAMES PARK

Photography by **HEAMI LEE**
Food styling by **PEARL JONES**
Prop styling by **GÖZDE EKER**

CHRONICLE BOOKS
SAN FRANCISCO

This book is dedicated to my amazing American parents, Princess and Lurch. I'm happy to use this book to let the world know how much I appreciate y'all for raising me.

Library of Congress Cataloging-in-Publication Data
Names: Park, James (Food writer), author. | Lee, Heami, photographer.
Title: Chili crisp : 50+ recipes to satisfy your spicy, crunchy, garlicky cravings /
James Park ; photography by Heami Lee ;
food styling by Pearl Jones ; prop styling by Gözde Eker.
Description: San Francisco : Chronicle Books, [2023] | Includes index. |
Identifiers: LCCN 2023003872 | ISBN 9781797219769 (hardcover)
Subjects: LCSH: Cooking (Hot pepper sauces) | Cooking, Chinese–Sichuan style. |
Cooking, Asian. | LCGFT: Cookbooks.
Classification: LCC TX819.H66 P37 2023 | DDC 641.6/384–dc23/eng/20230207
LC record available at https://lccn.loc.gov/2023003872https://lccn.loc.gov/2023003872

Manufactured in China.

Design by RACHEL HARRELL.
Photography by HEAMI LEE.
Food styling by PEARL JONES.
Prop styling by GÖZDE EKER.
Typesetting by FRANK BRAYTON.

Doritos is a registered trademark of FRITO-LAY NORTH AMERICA, INC. Fly By Jing is a registered trademark of Fly By Jing Inc. H Mart is a registered trademark of H Mart Companies, INC. Kewpie Mayo is a registered trademark of Kewpie Corporation. Lao Gan Ma is a registered trademark of Guiyang Nanming Laoganma Special Flavour Foodstuffs Co., Ltd. Lean Cuisine is a registered trademark of Societe des Produits Nestle S.A. Popeyes is a registered trademark of Popeyes Louisiana Kitchen, Inc. Shin Ramyun is a registered trademark of NONGSHIM CO., LTD. Spam is a registered trademark of Hormel Foods Corporation. Trader Joe's is a registered trademark of Trader Joe's Company. Twin Marquis is a registered trademark of Twin Marquis, Inc.

10 9 8 7 6 5

Chronicle books and gifts are available at special quantity discounts to corporations, professional associations, literacy programs, and other organizations. For details and discount information, please contact our premiums department at corporatesales@chroniclebooks.com or at 1-800-759-0190.

CHRONICLE BOOKS LLC
680 Second Street
San Francisco, California 94107
www.chroniclebooks.com

CONTENTS

Introduction

When I started writing a book about chili crisp, I had two thoughts. First, I was beyond thrilled that I could be as creative and wild as I wanted to be with my favorite condiment. I've always considered myself an unofficial chili crisp ambassador, recommending different chili crisps to my friends and introducing them to new, different ways to enjoy it. But, after all that excitement, I felt this immense pressure. I questioned whether I was the right person to write about chili crisp.

Chili crisp, or chili oil, is one of the most essential components of Chinese cuisine. And I am a Korean immigrant who's been living, cooking, and eating in America for over a decade, still learning about the enormous array of flavors of Chinese and Chinese American cooking. As someone who didn't grow up with chili crisp on my table, I was nervous about misrepresenting the rich history and personal meaning of this staple to many people who have been eating it since they were young.

Because chili crisp wasn't etched in my food memories and palate, as kimchi was in my life growing up, I was able to enjoy chili crisp, in its many forms and flavors, in my own nontraditional, boundary-pushing ways. I used that curiosity and enthusiasm to attempt to make my own version for the first time. To be perfectly honest, I didn't even think about developing my version of chili crisp until I started writing this book. There were already so many delicious options to choose from, so I didn't think there was a need for me to create my own. But, the first taste of my own chili crisp made me feel like I was on to something magical. It was spicy but not overpowering, savory yet balanced, and textured in a way that I could almost chew those chili flakes. I shared my version of chili

crisp and a few recipes that foregrounded the flavors of chili crisp with some serious eaters to get their feedback, and their praise and encouragement helped me feel like I needed to share my unconditional love for chili crisp through this book.

The tagline of one of my favorite chili crisp brands, Fly By Jing, is "Not traditional, but personal." I didn't think too much of it when I first read it. But, as I've been tasting what feels like gallons of chili crisp pretty much every day for months and constantly thinking about chili crisp, that sentence really hits me in a different way.

When I interviewed Jing Gao, the founder and CEO of Fly By Jing, a modern Asian food company that produces more than just delicious chili crisp, she shared her journey of starting to produce a condiment that wasn't as widely known as ketchup or hot sauce. Positioning it as a versatile, oil-based Chinese hot sauce with ingredients that Western consumers hadn't experienced before, Fly By Jing's Sichuan Chili Crisp was one of her ways of sharing her life story. Deeply inspired by her journey, I wanted to tell my own story with my chili crisp—not by starting a successful company, as Jing did, but by sharing, through this book, the joy and excitement that I feel in my kitchen.

I might not have grown up with fond memories of chili crisp, but my experiences and stories with it are just beginning. As I've been cooking and eating with chili crisp more than ever in my life, I'm constantly falling in love with its complex yet addictive flavors. I'm creating happy memories on my own as I'm cooking these recipes, and I hope that you will as well.

I used to look at chili crisp as one of my hobbies. I loved talking about it, trying new brands, and finding new, creative ways to incorporate them into my dishes. But, all of a sudden, it became personal, as if it were a part of my identity and who I was. In a way, it really has been. It has become a vessel and a platform to share my flavors, personal stories, and background. My versions of the condiment aren't traditional, but they're exciting, heartwarming, and delicious. **My goal for this book is for you to explore your own stories with chili crisp.**

I once thought that there was only one type of chili crisp. Then, while researching for this book, thanks to my wonderful friends and family, who validated the taste of my chili crisp but also my story behind it, I broke out of that box and accepted the versatility of chili crisp. I didn't need to worry about why so many versions tasted different or feel pressured to pick one or another, thinking that there was limited space for all of them. In reality, each jar of chili crisp deserves its spot in the pantry because of the personal stories each jar represents.

My chili crisp, thanks to the usage of Korean ingredients like gochujang and gochugaru, had flavors reminiscent of Korean cuisine, but wasn't quite Korean—similar to how I was born in Korea but don't feel quite Korean because I grew up in America. Other chili crisps would have different ingredients that set them apart from each other. Some would have more garlic, while others—especially Sze Daddy Taiwanese Chili Sauce from chef Eric Sze, the owner of 886, a popular Taiwanese restaurant in New York City—would blend all the ingredients into a paste.

Whether you are a chili crisp connoisseur or a newbie who has never bought your own jar before, you are tasting the joy, excitement, hope, and ambition of someone's life by using it. The best part is that this book will inspire you to create your own chili crisp so that you can start sharing your own stories, one jar of chili crisp at a time. Maybe you have a special connection with certain ingredients that will pair fantastically with chili flakes. Or you haven't found "the one" even after tasting so many different types of chili crisp. Tasting, cooking, and even making your own chili crisp can bring exciting opportunities to not only learn more about yourself but also share the wonderful flavors of your life.

The recipes in the book are inspired by a lot of different influences in my life. As a Korean immigrant who cooks lots of Korean food, I included a fair number of Korean-inspired dishes with chili crisp. You will be tasting and cooking parts of my life story, which I'm so incredibly honored to share with you. There are plenty of American classics in here, just with the "volume turned up" (or should I say, spice turned up), such as Skillet-Roasted Chili Crisp Chicken and Vegetables (page 101, inspired by my love for and fascination with Ina Garten), Fiery Spaghetti and Meatballs (page 70, my homage to one of my favorite comfort foods), Spicy Potato Gratin (page 129, my favorite Thanksgiving dish), Spicy Tahini Cream Cheese Swirled Brownies (page 149, my go-to dinner party dessert that always makes everyone happy), and so much more.

One of many reasons I love chili crisp is that a dollop of it brings everything to life. It's that sensation and taste that your tongue appreciates. It's the magic of how something that's just okay becomes something unforgettable. It's not an exaggeration to say that this condiment gives me life. When I make my Chili Crisp Fried Eggs (page 31) almost every morning, the incredible aroma that takes over the kitchen energizes me. I get emotional when people tell me how much they enjoy my chili crisp. I feel alive when its spice makes me sweaty. Chili crisp has become indispensable in my life, from eating my happy feelings to creating new meaningful connections with people over our mutual love of chili crisp. And, from my years of being vocal about my love of chili crisp online, I know there are a lot of other enthusiasts out there!

My goal with the book is to create a connection over our love of chili crisp. I hope you feel that sparkle of inspiration for the infinite ways to use chili crisp in your everyday cooking, as I did. I hope you feel empowered to incorporate chili crisp in recipes that you've never thought about before. And most important, I hope you become energized and joyful as you cook (and eat!) each recipe.

I want this book's focus to be the joy of discovering flavors of chili crisp, finding new, exciting ways to enjoy it, and lastly, sharing your own story by creating your perfect, personal chili crisp. You will go through lots of chili crisp as you are cooking through the book, and that jar you opened months ago will quickly be gone.

This book is a celebration of all things chili crisp, not an encyclopedia. I'm not here to lecture you; I am not your chili crisp professor! But I will share my knowledge about the condiment as your unofficial chili crisp hype man. Think of me as your overly enthusiastic friend who can't stop talking about chili crisp. I'm thrilled that we get to go on this spicy adventure together.

One of the most exciting and toughest parts of writing this book was testing all the recipes with as many different kinds of chili crisp as I could find. All chili crisps have different spice levels, oil amounts, and flavor profiles, and it was a little challenging to find the baseline that would work with any type. I hope you didn't think that the recipes in the book would work only with my recipe for Everday Savory Chili Crisp (page 18)! Each recipe is tested with multiple kinds of chili crisp (I already have dedicated shelves for all my jars!). It might not taste exactly like the version I developed in my kitchen, especially if you use a brand that

I didn't use, but that's what's exciting about cooking with chili crisp. It's never the same! So use whatever brand you can find to cook the recipes in this book. But, to make the cooking and eating experiences as standard as possible, I tested all of my recipes (except the desserts) with Lao Gan Ma Spicy Chili Crisp, one of the most accessible chili crisps you can find. With the ridiculous number of jars I went through, Lao Gan Ma should consider giving me a tour of their factory!

Of course, I think my chili crisp recipe will work the best, but I want to make sure that this book gives you a road map to how you can maximize your current chili crisp jars so that you can feel the joy of cooking with them.

As you cook your feelings throughout the book, you will discover how versatile this savory, fiery condiment is. Allow yourself to feel that joy and excitement of cooking with it. It's going to be one spicy road ahead of you.

Chili Crisp 101: *Everything to Know about the Savory, Flavorful, Sometimes Fiery Condiment*

What is chili crisp?

Chili crisp is an oily, textured condiment made from chili flakes. I've always thought of it as a spicy condiment, similar to sriracha and ketchup. But, Jing Gao, the founder of Fly By Jing, a modern Asian food company whose bestselling item is Sichuan Chili Crisp, shared another perspective that I hadn't thought of: "It's a popular type of Chinese hot sauce or chili sauce that's oil-based. It's textured, savory, umami, and complements a lot of flavors," says Jing. "It's a type of hot sauce. I like saying this because it shows that you don't have to be afraid to use it."

And I wholeheartedly agree with her about categorizing chili crisp as hot sauce, because it diversifies where it can be used. Nowadays, you can find hot sauce at any restaurant and in any pantry. I hope that one day I can ask for chili crisp wherever I go beyond Asian restaurants.

What are the main ingredients of chili crisp?

The main ingredients of chili crisp are a variety of chili flakes, seasonings, additional crispy ingredients, and oil. There are infinite possibilities of flavors and tastes because of these big umbrella categories. Even among chili flakes alone, there are hundreds of different types from different cultures, beyond just Chinese Sichuan chili flakes, one of the most commonly used for chili crisp. Other common ingredients include fermented black beans, fried garlic, fermented soybeans, and MSG.

What's the history of chili crisp?

There have always been spicy condiments, especially in Chinese cuisine. But Spicy Chili Crisp from Lao Gan Ma is one of the first brands that popularized the idea of chili crisp in China. The iconic Lao Gan Ma product was created by a woman named Tao Huabi in 1984. She made her version of chili crisp at her noodle shop in China's Guizhou Province. Eventually, in 1997, Tao began bottling her popular condiment and started the first mass production of it under Lao Gan Ma Special Flavor Foodstuffs Company in Guizhou. Lao Gan Ma's Spicy Chili Crisp quickly became an essential Chinese pantry staple. Today, about 1.3 million bottles of the sauce are produced daily to be sold in China, America, Australia, and more than thirty other countries, according to the company's website.

The popularity of Lao Gan Ma Spicy Chili Crisp inspired the renaissance of different varieties of chili crisp in America today. It's safe to say that without Lao Gan Ma's Spicy Chili Crisp, there wouldn't be the chili crisp boom that we know now.

Do all chili crisps taste similar?

Absolutely not! That's like saying all hot sauces taste the same. My good friend put it this way, which instantly clicked with me: It's like how not all kimchi tastes the same! Depending on what types of chili flakes, oil, seasonings, and additional ingredients are used, chili crisps can taste wildly

different from each other. Some might be super mild, while others may be oilier, or crunchier and spicier. The exciting options and wide range of flavors and textures of chili crisp are the reasons why I highly encourage you to try many different types to find your favorite and build your perfect chili crisp collection.

What's the difference between chili oil and chili crisp?

The main differences between chili oil and chili crisp are the components and the oil-to-crisp ratio. And the terms are not necessarily interchangeable. Chili crisp has chili oil, but chili oil doesn't have chili crisp. If that idea confuses your brain, let's break it down together.

Chili crisp refers to chili oil and crisp ingredients, such as chili flakes, fried garlic, fermented black beans, and so on. You should be able to taste and see the crisp textures. Some chili crisps contain more oil than others, but what constitutes chili crisp is the presence of crisp. In contrast, chili oil purely means oil, like olive oil and canola oil. It's simply chili-infused oil, so there are no visible flavoring agents.

What are some popular brands out there?

There seem to be more new brands making chili crisp every single day, and I wish I could taste all of them! Many chefs and popular restaurants have started to bottle their chili crisp to sell online, giving more delicious options to chili crisp fans like myself.

Some of the most notable popular brands that are easily accessible are Sichuan Chili Crisp from Fly By Jing, S&B Crunchy Garlic with Chili Oil, Momofuku Chili Crunch, Su Chili Crisp, KariKari Garlic Chili Crisp, and so much more! I mean, even Trader Joe's has a chili crisp called Crunchy Chili Onion!

How do I store it?

Depending on the types of chili crisp you get, you will have to refrigerate it or keep it in the pantry. I keep all my chili crisp in the fridge, even those that don't specifically call for refrigeration. I think the flavors keep longer in the fridge, but many varieties don't require refrigeration. For my Everyday Savory Chili Crisp (page 18), I recommend storing it in the fridge because there are cooked green onions and garlic.

How do I use it?

There are infinite ways to use chili crisp. The most basic uses include drizzling it over dumplings, noodles, pizza, pasta, and honestly anything you like to eat, including snacks like Doritos! Chocolate chips? Popcorn? Go wild!

If you only drizzle this on everything, you wouldn't need to buy a whole book about it, right? Wrong! That's why I'm here!

Whether you are a big chili crisp fan who has gone through countless jars or you have never heard of chili crisp until now, I want to shift the way we use and think of chili crisp. The overarching theory that I propose is that we need to think of chili crisp as more than a condiment—it's a lifestyle! While I'm only partially joking, I really mean that it's a part of seasoning and building a dish, as versatile as olive oil: You can use olive oil to sauté, but you can also drizzle it on top of pasta or salad. Depending on how you use it, the taste and experience change. And that's what we are going to do with this book! We are going on a spicy adventure together that will shatter your perceptions and misconceptions of what chili crisp can do (get ready for the dessert chapter, which might be the most questionable one for you!).

Essential Pantry Items

Having a well-stocked pantry is vital to cooking delicious foods all the time. Even if you don't have a lot of ingredients in the fridge, you can quickly build good flavors with pantry items. When I developed all the recipes for the book, I rarely used things outside of my standard pantry spices and seasonings. These items regularly appear throughout the book, and once you have them, you are all set to experience the chili crisp magic!

Aleppo Pepper

This is a common Middle Eastern spice known for its fruity, savory, smoky, and slightly spicy flavors. In the form of pepper flakes, Aleppo pepper is milder than other pepper flakes, including Sichuan pepper flakes. As one of the essential chili flakes used to make Everyday Savory Chili Crisp (page 18), it creates a gorgeous dark ruby color when it's infused with oil.

Black Vinegar

Unlike basic white vinegar, black vinegar adds not only acidity but also umami. As one of the flavoring ingredients for making chili crisp, it adds a beautiful funk with a slight sweetness. Its nuanced, not-so-aggressive acidity complements the spice of chili flakes wonderfully in chili crisp.

Chicken Bouillon Powder

As a flavor enhancer, often used for quick stock, chicken bouillon powder is a yellow, dry seasoning. It's salty and highly concentrated, so a little bit goes a long way. It often comes in a small canister and my go-to brand is Lee Kum Kee. Like chicken bouillon cubes, it brings intense chicken flavor when mixed with water. It often contains MSG, which brings a layer of umami as well.

Diamond Crystal Kosher Salt

There are a lot of different types of salt: Himalayan pink salt, sea salt, and coarse salt, just to name a few. And, depending on which salt you use, the recipe tastes drastically different. So, my choice of salt is always Diamond Crystal Kosher salt because it sticks to food easily and it's not overly salty. It's one of the most important pantry ingredients, and I highly recommend using this kosher salt if you don't have it already!

Fish Sauce

This liquid seasoning brings sharp, funky saltiness to dishes. The unique process of fermenting fish, such as anchovies, creates its unique salty flavors. It's fantastic for adding a lot of flavor to stir-fries and soups.

Fried Shallots

One of the main crisp ingredients for making Everyday Savory Chili Crisp (page 18), fried shallots have an ideal mild onion flavor while also providing a nice crunch. You can make fried shallots from scratch, but store-bought fried shallots are useful because they can be stored at room temperature without losing their crunch for a while.

Gochugaru

Gochugaru are Korean red pepper flakes. The spice level ranges from mild to hot, depending on the type of peppers. It's one of the essential spices responsible for creating spicy flavors in Korean cuisine. There are two types of gochugaru, coarse and fine. The fine powder is often used for making gochujang while the coarse is used for making kimchi. Coarse-ground gochugaru is ideal for general cooking, including making chili crisp.

Gochujang

Gochujang is a Korean red pepper paste. It's slightly sweet and spicy, which makes it ideal for seasoning broth, creating marinades, and infusing oil. Everyday Savory Chili Crisp (page 18) starts with gochujang-infused oil, creating a deep umami flavor.

Green Onions

If there's one ingredient that's used in pretty much every savory recipe throughout the book, it's green onions. Many dishes benefit from using a lot of them, whether as final garnishes or as aromatics in the beginning. Green onion–infused oil, also known as pa-gi-rum in Korean, creates a nice savory foundation of flavors in many recipes. One of the reasons why Everyday Savory Chili Crisp (page 18) is packed with umami is the green onion–infused oil. Since I go through so many green onions, I slice bundles of them and store them in an airtight container in the fridge. By doing so, I can easily use them for any purpose, from aromatics to final garnishes. One medium green onion, chopped, produces roughly 2 Tbsp.

Ground Ginger

Ground ginger has a more potent flavor than fresh ginger. It's one of my essential ingredients for making chili crisp. It's ideal for mixing with other spices.

Kewpie Mayo

This Japanese mayonnaise has unique tangy flavors. It's creamy and rich with a touch of sweetness. It's slightly yellower than traditional mayonnaise because of the inclusion of egg yolks. If you want to mimic the flavors of Kewpie mayo, mix regular mayo with a dash of rice wine vinegar and a little bit of sugar.

Kimchi

Kimchi is a catchall term for a Korean side dish of salted and fermented vegetables. Most commonly, it's made with napa cabbage or radish, and the usage of gochugaru, Korean red pepper flakes, colors the kimchi red. The older and more fermented the kimchi, the more sour it gets. When cooking with kimchi in dishes such as Dubu Jorim (page 121), if the kimchi isn't quite ripe, add a little bit of vinegar to mimic its flavors.

Mirin

Mirin is a rice wine that adds a punch of sweet and umami flavors. It's not high in alcohol compared to sake or any cooking wine. Commonly used for making glaze and sauces, mirin is especially essential when cooking meat and seafood.

Miso

Miso is a Japanese fermented soybean paste, a fantastic seasoning often used in soups and marinades. It's packed with umami and brings subtle, earthy, salty flavors. There are different types of miso available in different colors. Lighter colors are sweeter and mild in flavor, suitable for soups and dressings, while darker colors have a funkier, saltier flavor and are better for braises.

MSG

As a flavor enhancer, MSG contains the pure taste of umami. As a dry seasoning, it's a quick way to add a punch of flavors. It's an essential ingredient to make chili crisp savory.

Oyster Sauce

This seasoning is earthy, savory, sweet, and salty and is one of the most important seasonings. Contrary to its name, it's not fishy, and is ideal for stir-frying vegetables, noodles, and rice.

Panko

Made from crustless white bread that's processed into dried flakes, panko is a great way to add crisp textures. Whether used for dredging vegetables and proteins (such as in Panko-Crusted Baked Salmon, page 108) or sprinkling at the end to add more texture (such as in Creamy Rigatoni with Crispy Chickpeas, Spinach, and Lemony Panko, page 73), it's a must-have pantry item.

Pork Floss

Pork floss, also known as rousong, yuk sung, or meat floss, is a shredded, dried meat product that looks like cotton candy, except it's slightly salty and

savory. It has that intense meat flavor, reminiscent of meat jerky, with a hint of sweetness at the end. It's a delicious garnish on dishes like jook, or Savory Morning Oats with Jammy Eggs and Pork Floss (page 35), and is often used as a filling for sticky rice rolls, fan tuan.

Potato Starch

Extracted from potatoes, potato starch is one of many starch options along with cornstarch. It's often used as a thickening agent or dredge for proteins before frying. I prefer potato starch over cornstarch, especially when frying, because it creates a crisp texture due to its high-temperature tolerance. But, it can be swapped with more commonly found starch options, such as cornstarch, for recipes like Spicy Seafood Stir-Fry over Rice (page 111).

Rice Wine Vinegar

Rice wine vinegar is my go-to choice for adding acid. Compared to white distilled vinegar, which has sharp acidity, rice wine vinegar, or rice vinegar, is sweeter and relatively milder in acidic flavors. Acid, especially in many dishes with chili crisp, is important because it wakes up other flavors in the recipe. I use this a lot when making sauces with chili crisp throughout the book. It balances the spice and adds a subtle sweetness to sauces and marinades.

Sesame Seeds

There's a saying in Korean cuisine that a dish isn't complete without sprinkles of sesame seeds. They add a wonderful nutty crunch to any dish, especially when roasted, without overpowering it. They are also one of the essential ingredients of my Everyday Savory Chili Crisp (page 18), adding a nice texture and a pleasantly nutty flavor.

Sichuan Chili Flakes (Chinese Chili Powder)

Chinese Sichuan chili flakes are made from dried Chinese red peppers. Some common varieties include Facing Heaven chiles and Er Jing Tiao chiles. Depending on the brand and variety, the level of spice, flavors, and coarseness can change. Since they contribute all the spice to homemade chili crisp, choose the kind that has the desired heat level. Some Sichuan chili flakes are incredibly spicy, while others are darker in color and not as spicy, even less than regular Italian crushed red pepper flakes. I highly recommend trying different brands until you find one that works for your palate. For my Everyday Savory Chili Crisp (page 18), I use Natural Plus Green Sichuan Chili Flakes, available on Amazon.

Soy Sauce

There are so many different types of soy sauce on the market: low-sodium, gluten-free, and dark, just to name a few. Because all soy sauces have different flavors, you'll get different results depending on which soy sauce you use. For the recipes throughout the book, I used light soy sauce, ideal for all-purpose general cooking. It's fairly interchangeable with any all-purpose soy sauce, but be sure not to use dark soy sauce or any sweetened soy sauce.

Tapioca Flour (Tapioca Starch)

Tapioca flour is a secret ingredient in two of the recipes in this book: It's a fantastic gluten-free baking ingredient that makes the Spicy Green Onion Pancakes (page 143) super crispy and gives the Zesty Chili Crisp Focaccia (page 85) a one-of-a-kind, shatteringly crispy-crunchy texture. Made from the roots of the cassava plant, tapioca flour is extremely versatile, both in baking and in cooking. It doesn't have any taste or particular smell and can be used in anything without changing the texture and flavor.

Toasted Sesame Oil

Toasted sesame oil is one of the essential pantry items for Asian cooking. Its brown color, noticeably different from regular sesame oil, brings intensely toasty, nutty flavors to a dish. A little goes a long way, so don't overuse it. But a little dash of it, mixed in regular oil or chili crisp, such as for Chili Crisp Fried Eggs (page 31), makes a big difference.

ESSENTIAL CHILI CRISPS

Everyday Savory Chili Crisp

There are two essential things to consider when making the perfect chili crisp: the oil-to-crisp ratio and the flavor profiles. I decided that my ideal chili crisp would have more crisp than oil and different types of crunchy, savory fillings, such as fried shallots and chicken boullion powder. A unique blend of chili flakes creates complex and layered levels of heat. And, making an oil infused with gochujang, green onion, and garlic as a base creates a rich, beautiful red color for the oil. I highly recommend doubling the recipe so that it lasts even longer—believe me, you'll use it up faster than you think!

1. In a small saucepan, add 1 cup [240 ml] of the oil and the gochujang. Turn the heat to super low and cook, stirring occasionally, for 3 to 5 minutes, or until the gochujang starts to bubble and the oil darkens slightly. Add the green onions and cook for another 2 to 4 minutes, or until soft. Add the minced garlic, increase the heat to medium-low, and cook for 5 to 7 minutes, or until the onions and garlic are crisp and fragrant. Set aside.

2. While the oil is cooling, in an 8 in [20 cm] heatproof, preferably stainless steel, medium bowl, combine the gochugaru, Sichuan chili flakes, sesame seeds, Aleppo pepper flakes, sesame oil, chicken powder, sugar, salt, ginger, MSG, soy sauce, and vinegar.

3. Pour the infused oil directly into the bowl with the ingredients. Mix with a heatproof spatula so there are no lumps. There should not be any sizzle at this stage.

4. In the now-empty saucepan, add the remaining 1 cup [240 ml] of oil and heat over high heat for 3 minutes, or until the oil smokes. Carefully pour the hot oil into the bowl of the ingredients; the hot oil should sizzle as it hits the bowl. If the mixture doesn't sizzle, heat the oil in 30-second intervals.

5. Let the mixture sit for at least 5 minutes. Then, add the fried shallots and carefully mix everything again. Let the mixture come to room temperature and then transfer it to an airtight container. It can be stored in the fridge for about 3 months.

MAKES ABOUT 4 CUPS [860 G]

2 cups [480 ml] neutral oil, such as vegetable or canola

1 Tbsp gochujang

¾ cup [80 g] chopped green onions (4 to 6 medium)

6 to 8 garlic cloves, minced

5 Tbsp [40 g] gochugaru

5 Tbsp [40 g] Sichuan chili flakes

2 Tbsp sesame seeds

2 Tbsp Aleppo pepper flakes

1 Tbsp toasted sesame oil

1 Tbsp chicken bouillon powder (see Note)

1 Tbsp brown sugar

1 Tbsp kosher salt

1 tsp ground ginger

1 tsp MSG

3 Tbsp soy sauce

1 Tbsp black vinegar

½ cup [60 g] fried shallots

NOTE: To make it vegetarian, substitute the chicken powder with mushroom bouillon powder. You can omit the MSG, but I highly recommend it for an extra boost of umami flavors.

Very Nutty Chili Crisp

This chili crisp gets down to basics with only three components: oil, chili flakes, and crunch. Unlike Everyday Savory Chili Crisp (page 18), which is packed with complex, garlicky, umami flavors, Very Nutty Chili Crisp lets the texture of chopped nuts costar alongside the spice of chili flakes. It tastes super clean, with a pleasant amount of spice at the end, and the oil smells aromatic and deliciously nutty thanks to a blend of chopped nuts. After testing Lao Gan Ma, one of my favorite chili crisps, in my dessert recipes with unpleasant results, I came up with this chili crisp specifically to complement desserts. It has a little bit of umami from fried chili flakes, so a dollop of this will really elevate the taste of sweets. I honestly swear by using Very Nutty Chili Crisp whenever I make desserts. You can, of course, use this for savory dishes, such as biscuits or noodles. But the best dish to use this chili crisp that made me roll my eyes in flavor pleasure? Spicy Tahini Cream Cheese Swirled Brownies (page 149).

MAKES ABOUT 2½ CUPS [600 G]

5 Tbsp [40 g] gochugaru

5 Tbsp [40 g] Sichuan chili flakes

2 Tbsp Aleppo pepper flakes

1 Tbsp light brown sugar

1½ tsp kosher salt

1 cup [140 g] coarsely chopped nuts (see Notes)

1½ cups [360 ml] neutral oil, such as vegetable or canola

1. In a heatproof medium bowl, combine the gochugaru, Sichuan chili flakes, Aleppo pepper flakes, sugar, and salt. Set aside.

2. In a dry small saucepan over medium heat, toast the chopped nuts for 3 to 5 minutes, or until lightly browned but not completely dark. Add the toasted nuts to the bowl with the spices.

3. In the same small saucepan over high heat, add the oil and heat for 3 minutes, or until lightly smoking.

4. Carefully drizzle the hot oil into the bowl of nuts and spices. Let the hot oil sizzle for the flavors to bloom. If it doesn't sizzle, heat the oil in 30-second intervals. Let it sit for 5 minutes, then mix everything together. Let the mixture come to room temperature, then transfer it to an airtight container. It can be stored in the fridge about 3 months. You can store it at room temperature, but for longer storage, keep it in the refrigerator.

NOTES: The best way to coarsely chop nuts is to pulse them in a food processor. Be careful not to turn them into a paste. Nuts should be coarse to provide a nutty texture to the chili crisp.

When it comes to the types of nuts for this chili crisp, you can use any type of nuts you want, such as peanuts, walnuts, almonds, pistachios, pine nuts, and even pecans. The possibilities are endless! Use either one type of nut or a mixture of different nuts.

If you are allergic to any types of nuts, replace them with any types of seeds, like pumpkin seeds or sesame seeds.

Garlicky Onion Crunch

As one of many Trader Joe's superfans, I was particularly excited when I found out about their version of chili crisp, called Crunchy Chili Onion. It's not spicy compared to common chili crisps, such as Fly By Jing's, but it is textured and filled with lots of crispy bits. It is garlicky, oniony, and crunchy, as the name suggests, and for that, it earned a spot in my ever-growing chili crisp collection.

I wanted to create a copycat version inspired by its insanely crunchy, not-so-spicy flavor notes. There are no gochugaru or Sichuan chili flakes here, because this chili crisp is not meant to be spicy. Red pepper flakes alone bring a welcoming level of heat, and Aleppo pepper brings a nice color and depth to this chili crisp.

This chili crisp is the best version to use as a garnish due to its simple ingredients. Put this on top of Cheesy Cornbread with Green Chiles (page 88) or Zesty Chili Crisp Focaccia (page 85) to add a nice crunch.

MAKES ABOUT 1½ CUPS [400 G]

1 cup [240 ml] olive oil

½ cup [55 g] dehydrated minced onion

¼ cup [40 g] minced garlic

2 to 3 Tbsp red pepper flakes

2 Tbsp Aleppo pepper flakes

1 Tbsp soy sauce

1 Tbsp smoked paprika

1 Tbsp kosher salt

1. In a deep skillet or saucepan over low heat, add the olive oil, dehydrated minced onion, and minced garlic. Heat for 6 to 8 minutes, or until the onion and garlic get toasty and brown.

2. Add the red pepper flakes and Aleppo pepper flakes and cook for about 1 minute, stirring constantly.

3. Transfer the mixture to a heatproof bowl. Add the soy sauce, paprika, and salt and stir to combine. Let it cool for 5 to 10 minutes before transferring it to an airtight container and store for up to 3 months.

Garlicky Onion Crunch (page 20)

Very Nutty Chili Crisp (page 19)

Everyday Savory Chili Crisp (page 18)

Your Perfect Chili Crisp Formula

Chili Flakes

This is arguably one of the most important components of making chili crisp. It sets the tone for flavors and heat level, and it creates the unique identity of chili crisps. It's important not to use chili powder for this because we want to *see* chunks of chili flakes. The coarser the flakes, the better. If you can't find chili flakes, I would recommend getting dried chiles and breaking them apart in a food processor. You can just use one kind, but I highly recommend playing with a blend of different varieties to maximize flavors. Following, I provide a list of chili flakes with a range of Scoville Heat Units (SHU), a metric to understand how spicy each pepper is. This number is measured by the number of times capsaicin, the main component that makes peppers spicy, needs to be diluted by sugar-water. It ranges anywhere from 0 to millions!

Maybe you've tasted a few different types of chili crisp but haven't found "the one" yet. Don't worry; I'm here to guide you in making your perfect chili crisp formula. When making chili crisp, there are three main components—chili flakes, oil, and flavoring—and the combinations are infinite. You can customize the flavors, textures, and spices that satisfy your chili crisp fantasy.

Let's go on this adventure together, shall we?

Aleppo Pepper Flakes (about 10,000 SHU)

These Middle Eastern pepper flakes are lightly smoky and moderately spicy but not over-powering. They create a deep, dark color when infused in oil.

Ancho Dried Chili Flakes (500–3,000 SHU)

These have a deeply fruity taste, like dried plums and sweet raisin, with a touch of smoke. If used in making chili crisp, the color will be slightly different from the traditional, dark-red color because the flakes are more brown.

Cobanero Chili Flakes (30,000–50,000 SHU)

These Guatemalan chili flakes have bright, smoky, and sweet fla-vors and definitely bring the heat.

Gochugaru (4,000–8,000 SHU)

These Korean red pepper flakes are slightly fruity and not super spicy. Gochugaru builds a nice savory taste when used in chili crisp.

Guajillo Dried Chili Flakes (2,500–5,000 SHU)

These herbaceous, delicate chili flakes have a wonderful balance of ripe fruits and tingles of fresh peppers.

Pasilla Chili Flakes (250–4,000 SHU)

These Mexican chili flakes have slightly nutty, fruity flavors.

Red Jalapeño Chili Flakes (7,500–10,000 SHU)

Did you know that there are red jalapeño peppers? These chili flakes bring a nice kick of spice to many dishes.

Red Pepper Flakes (30,000–50,000 SHU)

As the vague name suggests, these chili flakes aren't from any specific type of peppers. They include all parts of the pepper, including skin and veins. Don't underestimate how spicy, some-times sharp, they can be.

Sichuan Pepper Flakes (50,000–75,000 SHU)

Sichuan pepper flakes can be made with a variety of dried peppers, including small "Facing Heaven" peppers or Er Jing Tiao chili, a slightly milder version that's considered Sichuan Province's most-loved chile pepper.

Silk Chili Flakes (5,000–10,000 SHU)

These Turkish chili flakes have a pleasant, tomato-like flavor with a moderate level of spice, similar to Aleppo pepper flakes.

Oil

Oil transforms chili flakes into chili crisp. It doesn't add dramatic flavors to the overall product, but a good blend of oil can add subtle differences that will make your chili crisp unique. One important note: You have to think about the smoke point. Depending on the type of oil you choose, you may not be able to simmer chili flakes in oil for as long as you would like, because the hot temperature of the oil may burn the chili flakes too quickly. The point here is to have fun and find your own perfect oil through trial and error, so think beyond just canola oil and olive oil. How about ghee? Margarine? Beef fat? Any sort of liquid fat will work here. I'm imagining a chili crisp made out of chicken fat—I haven't made that yet, but imagine how wildly delicious that would be!

- Avocado oil
- Beef fat
- Canola oil
- Chicken fat
- Coconut oil
- Duck fat
- Ghee
- Grapeseed oil
- Olive oil
- Peanut oil
- Sesame oil
- Vegetable oil

Flavoring

This is the part where things get interesting and creative. This element is where you can add your own twist. Whether it's for adding textures, such as fried garlic, or flavors, such as black vinegar, the unwritten rule of flavoring chili crisp is to keep the options open and exciting. Maybe you want to add potato chips for crunch! Or crushed chicken skin? The sky's the limit!

- Apple cider vinegar
- Black vinegar
- Brown sugar
- Chicken bouillon powder
- Crushed almonds
- Crushed peanuts
- Dried onion
- Fried garlic
- Fried onion
- Fried shallots
- Gochujang
- Miso
- MSG
- Mushroom bouillon powder
- Pomegranate molasses
- Soy sauce
- Toasted sesame seeds
- Tomato paste

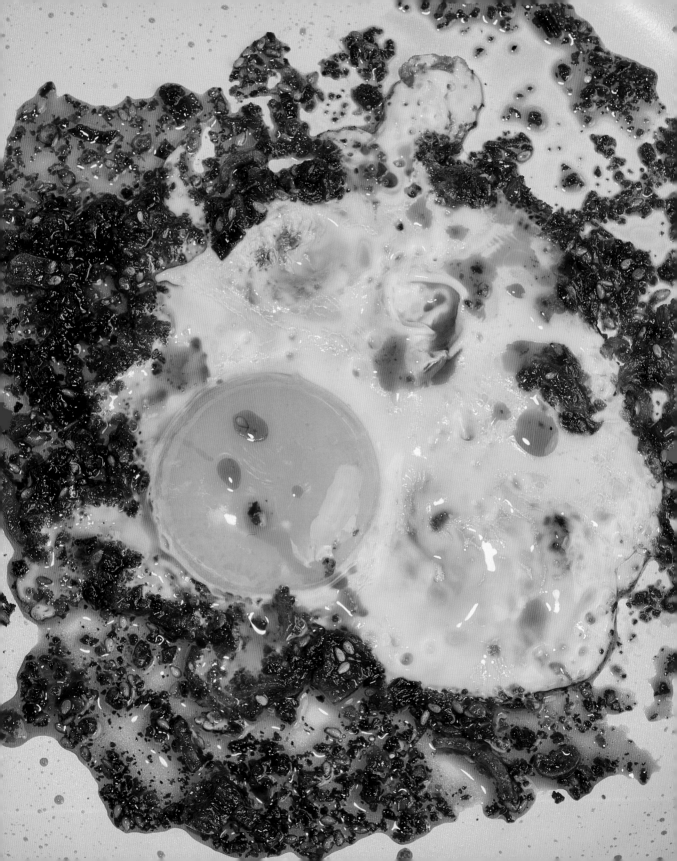

chapter 1

ALL-DAY BREAKFAST AND MIDDAY SNACKS

MY DREAMY CHILI CRISP PAIRING

There was a distinct moment that unleashed my wild chili crisp imagination, and it involved crispy fried chicken, specifically Popeyes'. It was just a regular night of eating my feelings and treating myself with Popeyes fried chicken. I was thinking of the other delicious ways I could enjoy this box of crispy goodness. After looking at the box of biscuits, mashed potatoes, and a stack of big pieces of Popeyes chicken, I had a light bulb moment and started building my perfect bite.

I split open that warm, buttery biscuit. Then, I smeared on a generous scoop of mashed potatoes, as if I were frosting a cupcake. Instead of simply adding pieces of chicken, I took a whole layer of crunchy fried chicken skin from one of the big pieces and layered it on top of the mashed potatoes. I was ready to close the top to enjoy this perfection, then I remembered: a jar of chili crisp in my fridge. I quickly ran to the fridge, opened my precious jar of chili crisp, and doused the chicken skin generously, letting it seep into the nooks and crannies. I finally took a bite, and it truly sent me to fried chicken heaven. Buttery biscuits, creamy mashed potatoes, and insanely crunchy chicken skin checked off everything that I was looking for in one mind-blowing bite, but what really connected all of them was a drizzle of chili crisp. The savory and spicy flavors elevated all the components just enough to make this bite truly unforgettable.

Ever since that life-changing moment, I can't eat fried chicken without chili crisp. It's one of my dreamiest chili crisp pairings, but there are other endless combinations that would take you to flavor heaven. Here are some of my absolute favorites.

6-Minute Jammy Eggs

Chili crisp is fantastic with any form of eggs: crispy fried eggs, hard-boiled eggs, sous vide eggs, scrambled eggs, omelets, you name it. But my absolute favorite is jammy 6-minute soft-boiled eggs. The rich, runny yolk completes the flavor equation with chili crisp in my opinion. Try my Spicy Egg Salad Sandwich (page 40) to taste this dreamy pairing.

Bacon, Egg, and Cheese

Crispy bacon, fluffy eggs, and melty cheese, all sandwiched in a bagel is my favorite hangover cure. But imagine adding a dollop of chili crisp on top. It balances the wonderfully greasy bite with spice, and it instantly wakes you up.

Biscuits

Imagine warm, freshly baked, flaky biscuits with a smear of butter and a dollop of chili crisp. The warmth of the biscuits melts the butter nicely, and the chili crisp mixes with the butter, seeping into the biscuit crumb. This dreamy pairing is a must-try. Or incorporate chili crisp into your biscuit dough, as in the Chili Crisp Biscuits with Honey-Butter Glaze (page 44).

Cacio e Pepe

Cheese, ground black pepper, and carbs! Each element of this pasta dish is ideal for chili crisp. In general, any type of pasta is great with chili crisp, but I particularly enjoy chili crisp on cacio e pepe because of its strong peppery taste, which beautifully complements the chili flakes in chili crisp.

Cheeseburgers

Grilled meat patties with melty cheese? Both are screaming for chili crisp. Open the burger top, add a scoop of chili crisp right on top of the melty cheese, close the bun, and enjoy a heavenly bite.

Green Onion Pancakes

Any type of savory pancake is fantastic with chili crisp, but especially green onion pancakes. The crispy exterior of hot-off-the-skillet pancakes gently warms up the flavors of chili crisp, culminating in one of the most delicious bites. Try Spicy Green Onion Pancakes (page 143) to taste the deliciousness.

Jook (Congee)

Jook, or congee, is one of my favorite comfort foods. Because it's minimally seasoned, condiments like chili crisp are essential. A drizzle of chili crisp adds a ton of flavors and much-needed textures to this comfort food. For an easy spin-off, try a bowl of warm rice with chili crisp and a dash of soy sauce and toasted sesame oil.

Pork Belly (Samgyupsal)

Whether it's grilled, boiled, steamed, or simply sautéed, pork belly loves chili crisp. My go-to pairing is a grilled pork belly, done Korean barbecue style and dipped in chili crisp with thinly sliced raw garlic. It makes my eyes roll in pleasure every time. Try Spicy Pork Belly Stir-Fry with Celery (page 107) to understand why pork belly loves chili crisp.

Potato chips

One of my simplest pleasures is potato chips with a dollop of chili crisp. Salty, crunchy potatoes are a perfect fit for spicy chili crisp. This condiment can go with any type of potatoes, such as baked potatoes, crispy fries, hash browns, and more. Try Spicy Potato Gratin (page 129), which proves why chili crisp and potatoes belong together.

Silken Tofu

This pairing happens to be one of my favorite summer dishes. Just a block of cold silken tofu, a generous drizzle of chili crisp and soy sauce, and lots of fresh green onions on top. It's so refreshing and flavorful. When it's too hot outside to turn on the oven, or you want a quick side dish that you can put together in less than 10 minutes, this is the chili crisp pairing you need.

BUILD YOUR CHILI CRISP COLLECTION

I don't think there's only one soulmate or one perfect match for me in this world. And that's especially true when it comes to chili crisp. There are so many different types and varieties of chili crisp to try, so why should you limit yourself? I have about ten different types of chili crisp in my fridge, and I love all of them equally. Each chili crisp jar from my collection brings different types of joy. Some are more ideal for fried chicken; others are a better fit for pasta. It feels a bit like matchmaking to pair dishes with chili crisp.

I encourage you to build your perfect chili crisp collection. The more you try different kinds, the better you will understand your preferences. Be curious and adventurous when pairing this condiment with dishes. The same dumpling, for example, can be transformed into multiple flavor experiences depending on the type of chili crisp you drizzle on it. That's chili crisp's magic power!

After all, we should be curious about the stories and flavors that go into making chili crisp. Look into what makes a particular variety different from one you may have already tried. Think about the joy you will feel from trying the new chili crisp. Where do you see these flavors complementing your daily cooking? Adding a new jar of chili crisp to my collection is a way for me to get fresh perspectives, life stories, and flavors into my kitchen. And once I shifted my mindset from hoarding chili crisp jars to creating a story about different people's lives through chili crisp, my chili crisp collection became more than just my obsession: It became a part of my pride.

Chili Crisp Fried Eggs

MAKES 2 EGGS

1 Tbsp chili crisp

1 tsp toasted sesame oil

2 large eggs

Furikake, for garnish (optional)

Green onions, chopped, for garnish (optional)

Spicy, bright-red chili crisp adds so much flavor to simple fried eggs. It's one of the first dishes that made me fall in love with all the possibilities of cooking with chili crisp, beyond just as a finishing touch. Mixing chili crisp with a little bit of toasted sesame oil adds an extra layer of nutty flavor that takes crispy eggs to the next level. I recommend cooking eggs sunny-side up to make the yolk a rich sauce that complements the spicy chili crisp. Once you make this, you will never want to go back to frying eggs in plain oil.

1. In a medium skillet or sauté pan, preferably nonstick, over medium-low heat, warm the chili crisp and sesame oil. Gently crack the eggs over the chili crisp and let the eggs crisp up around the edges for 3 to 5 minutes, or until the whites are set but the yolk is still runny. Be sure to keep the heat medium-low to prevent the chili crisp from burning.

2. Enjoy chili crisp fried eggs on their own. Or serve them over toast, English muffins, or rice, which is a go-to, easy meal. Garnish with furikake and freshly chopped green onions, if desired. Feel free to add an extra drizzle of chili crisp on top of the fried eggs if you like.

NOTE: A chili crisp fried egg is an easy way to turn your boring rice into something incredible. Add 1 Tbsp of butter and 1 tsp of soy sauce to a bowl of cooked hot rice, and then slide the egg on top. Garnish with green onions, toasted sesame seeds, more chili crisp, and toasted sesame oil, if you want.

Whipped Ricotta Toast
with Spicy Tomato Confit

One of my favorite savory toasts is ricotta toast, and tomato confit with ricotta is my favorite ricotta flavor combination. The garlicky oil from the tomato confit uplifts and complements the creamy texture of ricotta, and the baked tomatoes ooze with a delightful sweetness. The addition of chili crisp provides just the right amount of heat without overpowering the tomatoes. You can serve tomato confit with plain ricotta straight out of the tub, but taking the extra step to whip the ricotta in a food processor to make it extra creamy is well worth the effort.

MAKES 2 TOASTS

2 cups [320 g] cherry tomatoes

¼ cup [60 ml] plus 1 Tbsp extra-virgin olive oil

2 Tbsp chili crisp

1 tsp toasted sesame oil

1 tsp granulated sugar

1 tsp kosher salt

2 tsp balsamic vinegar

2 garlic cloves, minced

¼ cup [60 g] ricotta

2 slices bread, preferably sourdough

Drizzle of honey for garnish

Flaky sea salt, for garnish

1. Preheat the oven to 325°F [165°C]. In a small bowl, combine the tomatoes, ¼ cup [60 ml] of the olive oil, chili crisp, sesame oil, sugar, salt, balsamic vinegar, and minced garlic. Toss everything to make sure that the tomatoes are well coated. Transfer the tomatoes to a 2 qt [2 L] baking dish. Bake in the oven for 1 hour and 30 minutes, or until the tomatoes are well cooked and bubbling. Let it cool for 20 minutes, or until just warm.

2. Add the ricotta and the remaining 1 Tbsp olive oil to a food processor and blend until smooth, or about 1 minute.

3. Toast the bread until golden brown and let cool slightly before topping generously with the ricotta. Add the spicy tomato confit on top of the whipped ricotta. Finish with a drizzle of honey and a sprinkle of flaky sea salt. The leftover tomato confit can be stored in an airtight container in the fridge for up to 1 week, and the whipped ricotta can be stored in an airtight container in the fridge for up to 2 days. Both can be reused right away to assemble the toast.

NOTE: You can rewarm leftover tomato confit in the microwave, but it's wonderful cold straight from the fridge. Because the recipe makes more than enough for the ricotta toast, here are some fun ways to eat up the leftovers besides making more toast: Toss it with cooked pasta to make a quick weeknight dinner. Mix it with cream cheese to make your breakfast bagel extra savory. Serve it with salad. Put it on top of burrata. Or simply eat it plain with a spoon, which is my favorite.

Spicy Breakfast Casserole *with* Tater Tots

Let's set the scene. You have a big, hungry crowd to feed for breakfast. Maybe it's the morning of a big family gathering. Or it's a morning after a crazy night with your crew at a getaway Airbnb. You want to make something hearty, cheesy, savory, crispy, and also a little bit spicy. That's where this big spicy breakfast casserole comes in to save the day.

This casserole has layers of different flavors. The first step is browning hot Italian sausage. Then all the aromatics and vegetables get cooked and coated with spicy sausage fat. You can eat this as is, but a fluffy egg mixture, made extra tangy with sour cream, transforms this into the ultimate hefty breakfast for a crowd. Chili crisp is used to season the eggs, sausage, and vegetables, adding more depth to each layer.

Oh, did I mention the best part of the dish? A layer of tater tots!! I mean, this dish calls for a whole bag of frozen tater tots: What a treat, right? Ever since I learned that you could line up tater tots to create a layer almost like a puzzle when building a casserole, I started to embrace my love for the crispy potatoes again. The final product is a visually stunning, showstopping dish with a party of flavors and textures in each corner. Each bite is guaranteed to have golden-brown, crispy tater tots, followed by a creamy, flavorful, slightly spicy egg mixture that tastes like weekend breakfast heaven.

You can make this in a traditional casserole dish, but I love assembling it in the same pan I cook the sausage in. Why dirty another dish when you can make this recipe into a one-pan wonder?

SERVES 10 TO 12

2 lb [910 g] hot Italian sausage

1 Tbsp neutral oil, such as vegetable or canola

1 medium yellow onion, diced

1 jalapeño pepper, diced

4 green onions, chopped

5 oz [140 g] baby spinach

Pinch of kosher salt

4 Tbsp [60 g] chili crisp, plus more for drizzling

8 large eggs

1 cup [240 g] sour cream

¼ cup [60 ml] milk

1 cup [80 g] shredded mozzarella cheese

1 cup [80 g] shredded Cheddar cheese

2 lb [910 g] frozen tater tots

1. Preheat the oven to 375°F [190°C].

2. Take the Italian sausage out of its casing. In a 12 in [30 cm] cast-iron or large ovenproof skillet or sauté pan over medium-high heat, add the oil and Italian sausage and cook for 3 to 5 minutes, or until the sausage starts to render its fat.

Add the onion and jalapeño pepper and cook for another 2 to 4 minutes, or until they begin to soften. Reserve about 1 Tbsp of the green parts of the green onions for garnish. Add the rest of the chopped green onion and the spinach to the skillet. Cook for a few minutes, or until the spinach is wilted and mix with the rest

of the vegetables and the sausage. Season with a pinch of salt and 2 Tbsp of the chili crisp. Sauté everything for a few minutes, or until fragrant, and spread everything into an even layer with a spatula. Turn off the heat and set it aside while working on the egg mixture.

cont'd.

3. In a large bowl, crack the eggs. Add the sour cream, milk, remaining 2 Tbsp of chili crisp, a pinch of salt, and about half of the mozzarella and Cheddar to the bowl. Whisk to combine.

4. Pour the egg mixture into the skillet with the cooked vegetables and sausage.

5. Arrange the frozen tater tots on top of the egg mixture in a single, even layer. Some tater tots will sink into the egg mixture, which is fine.

6. Bake for 40 to 45 minutes, or until the egg mixture is cooked and the tater tots are crispy and golden brown. Remove from the oven. Sprinkle the remaining mozzarella and Cheddar on top of the tater tots layer. Return to the oven for 5 minutes, or until the cheese is fully melted.

7. Garnish with the reserved 1 Tbsp of chopped green onions and an extra drizzle of chili crisp. Serve immediately. The leftovers can be stored in the fridge for 3 to 4 days.

Savory Morning Oats *with* Jammy Eggs *and* Pork Floss

SERVES 1

2 large eggs

1 cup [240 ml] broth of your choice or water

2 Tbsp chili crisp, plus more for drizzling

2 tsp miso

1 tsp soy sauce

½ cup [50 g] old-fashioned rolled oats

1 tsp toasted sesame oil

1 green onion, chopped, for garnish

Pork floss, for garnish

I still remember my first time trying oatmeal when I came to America. As a Korean immigrant, I was pretty used to a typical Korean breakfast, which consisted of rice, soup, and at least four different types of banchan. I was baffled when I learned Americans would eat just a bowl of bland oats. It didn't have any flavors. I would rather eat waffles!

Then, later in my adulthood, I came across savory oats. That's when I realized that it's not that oatmeal tasted bad, it just wasn't prepared properly! Say goodbye to your plain, regular beige oatmeal, and say hello to this savory, spicy orange oatmeal, which will revive your palate and soul in the morning. Many people finish oatmeal with a drizzle of chili crisp, but the key difference for this oatmeal recipe is that you make the flavorful broth in which you will cook the oats, which gives the oatmeal more profound, robust flavors. Other umami-forward ingredients like soy sauce and miso help balance the heat of chili crisp.

Oatmeal is just like jook or congee if you think about it—a blank canvas that can absorb any type of flavors and be as bland or as flavorful as you want. Soft-boiled, jammy eggs and pork floss are my forever go-to toppings for jook, and they certainly belong on my savory oats. Feel free to add other tasty toppings like toasted seaweed or kimchi. It's hearty, spicy, and satisfying and so versatile that it can easily be your delicious lunch, dinner, or midnight snack.

1. Fill a medium pot about three-quarters full with water and bring it to a boil. Prepare a bowl of ice water.

2. Carefully drop the eggs into the boiling water and let cook for 6½ minutes for soft-boiled, runny yolks. If you want your yolks to be slightly cooked but still somewhat jammy, cook for 7 minutes.

3. When the eggs are done cooking, transfer them to the ice water to shock and stop cooking. Set aside while making the oats.

cont'd.

4. In the same pot over medium-high heat, heat the broth. Once it simmers, add the chili crisp, miso, and soy sauce. Mix to combine. Add the oats, stir, and turn the heat to low. Simmer for 4 to 6 minutes while stirring occasionally, until the oats absorb most of the liquid and they look like a porridge.

5. Peel the soft-boiled eggs. Set them aside.

6. Transfer the cooked oatmeal to a bowl. Drizzle with the toasted sesame oil. Garnish with the peeled eggs, chopped green onions, and pork floss. Finish with a drizzle of chili crisp, if desired, and serve.

Kimchi Quesadilla
with Chili Crisp

Whenever I make quesadillas, I always add a drizzle of chili crisp on top. It might be messy, but it's the perfect spicy kick to cut through the cheesy goodness. But what about chili crisp inside the quesadilla filling as well? And tangy kimchi? All of my favorite flavor combos are in this ridiculously satisfying snack. You can use chopped kimchi, but it gets even better when it is cooked and slightly caramelized. Then, it gets dressed with chili crisp, umami-heavy soy sauce, and a little bit of sugar to balance the acidity. You can also mix this delicious kimchi filling with rice and call it a day.

1. In a large sauté pan or skillet over medium-high heat, heat 1 Tbsp of the neutral oil. Add the green onions and cook for 45 to 60 seconds, or until fragrant. Add the kimchi, chili crisp, soy sauce, sugar, and sesame oil to the pan. Cook everything for 3 to 5 minutes, or until the kimchi is slightly caramelized and all the liquid is evaporated. Turn off the heat, and let cool slightly.

2. In a large bowl, add the mozzarella cheese. Transfer the cooked kimchi to the bowl and stir to combine thoroughly.

3. Spread a third (or half, depending on how much filling you prefer) of the kimchi-mozzarella mixture onto a tortilla and fold the tortilla in half. Repeat the process with the remaining tortillas.

4. Wipe down the skillet and add the remaining 1 Tbsp of oil over medium-low heat. Once the oil is hot, add a folded tortilla to the pan and cook for 1 to 2 minutes on each side while pressing down with a spatula, until golden brown and crisp and the cheese mixture is fully melted. Repeat with the remaining quesadillas. Cut each in half and serve immediately. The leftovers can be stored in the fridge for up to 3 days and in the freezer for up to 2 months. To reheat the refrigerated leftovers, bake them in the oven at 400°F [200°C] for 5 to 8 minutes, or until the cheese is fully melted and the tortillas get crispy. You can also reheat quesadillas in the air fryer at the same temperature for the same amount of time.

MAKES 2 OR 3 QUESADILLAS

2 Tbsp neutral oil, such as vegetable or canola

⅓ cup [16 g] chopped green onions

1 cup [300 g] napa cabbage kimchi, chopped

2 Tbsp chili crisp

1 Tbsp soy sauce

1½ tsp granulated sugar

1½ tsp sesame oil

2 cups [160 g] low-moisture shredded mozzarella cheese

Two or three 8 in [20 cm] flour or corn tortillas

NOTE: I made this vegetarian-friendly, but you can add protein, such as leftover rotisserie chicken, crispy bacon, and more to make it a little heartier.

Spicy Egg Salad Sandwich

As a big fan of mayo, I've always enjoyed eating (and making) egg salad. Hard-boiled eggs, smashed with creamy mayo with sprinkles of sugar for a subtle sweetness at the end, are sandwiched in between cloudlike slices of milk bread. It's genuinely one of the most satisfying snacks, perfect at any given time of the day, whether it's at 1 p.m. as a lunch or 1 a.m. after a night of drinking.

Thanks to a spicy, umami-forward chili crisp, the white-and-yellow egg salad turns a beautiful jewellike orange color. The mayo and smashed egg tame the spice from chili crisp, making each bite irresistible. I am a big fan of having both soft-boiled eggs and hard-boiled eggs in my egg sandwich, but if you want to keep it simple, you can skip creating a cross-section of soft-boiled eggs. It may take a few trials to nail restaurant-level presentation, but don't give up! The feeling of joy and accomplishment when you finally see the runny yolk in the center with scoops of orange-toned spicy egg salad is truly indescribable.

MAKES 2 SANDWICHES

8 large eggs

¼ cup [60 g] Kewpie mayo

2 green onions, chopped

2 Tbsp chili crisp

1 tsp granulated sugar

1 tsp rice wine vinegar

½ tsp kosher salt

¼ tsp freshly ground black pepper

4 slices Japanese milk bread

1. Fill a medium pot with water and bring to a boil. Once the water boils, add the eggs to the pot. While the eggs are cooking, prepare two separate bowls with ice-cold water. Cook the eggs for 7½ minutes, and take out two of them. Put them in one of the prepared ice baths to shock and stop cooking. Cook the rest of the eggs for 1½ minutes more, for a total of 9 minutes. Once they are done, transfer them to the second ice bath. Let them rest in the cold water for at least 10 minutes before peeling.

2. In a small bowl, mix the mayo, green onions, chili crisp, sugar, vinegar, salt, and pepper. Set aside.

3. After 10 minutes, peel each batch of eggs while partially submerging them in the water. Shake off the excess water, then halve the soft-boiled eggs lengthwise. The yolk should be creamy and slightly jammy but not runny. Set aside. Roughly chop the 9-minute eggs into small pieces. Fold the chopped eggs into the dressing using a fork, breaking apart any big chunks. Taste and season with more salt if necessary. Set aside.

4. Lay flat two slices of milk bread. Place two soft-boiled egg halves, yolk-side down, in the center of each slice. Scoop roughly ½ cup [70 g] of the egg salad mixture on top of the soft-boiled eggs. Carefully spread the egg salad around the soft-boiled eggs to cover the entire surface of the bread. Top with the remaining bread slices and gently press down.

5. Rotate the sandwiches 90 degrees, and cut them in half. The cross-section should reveal the soft-boiled eggs. Serve immediately. The spicy egg salad mixture can be stored in an airtight container in the refrigerator for up to 3 days. You can also use it as a salad topping.

Chili Crisp Fried Rice

SERVES 2 OR 3

What's better than delicious fried rice? Combining two types of fried rice flavors and techniques into one excellent fried rice dish! Even if you don't think you need another recipe for fried rice, give this a try.

This dish is what happens when golden fried rice and garlic fried rice have a baby. It uses the techniques for making golden fried rice, where you separate the eggs and mix the yolks into the rice directly with seasonings before frying. The egg yolks coat each grain of rice, and when it gets tossed with plenty of oil, the texture of the rice gets airy, light, and almost glossy.

Then, like garlic fried rice, there's about ⅓ cup [40 g] of minced garlic in this recipe (and that's a lot of garlic!). The oil, infused with garlic and green onions, becomes a fantastic base for the yolk-seasoned rice. When I first took a bite of this, I felt like an anime character who tasted a bowl of life-changing fried rice as he was flying around the moon. The texture of yolk-coated rice, the spicy-umami flavors from chili crisp and oyster sauce, and the final garnish of crumbled toasted seaweed create a perfect flavor triangle.

You will find yourself opening your eyes wide after the first bite. And always, feel free to drizzle extra chili crisp on top!

3 large eggs

2 cups [360 g] cooked white short-grain rice

3 Tbsp chili crisp

2 tsp toasted sesame oil

1 Tbsp oyster sauce

1 tsp soy sauce

½ tsp kosher salt

3 Tbsp neutral oil, such as vegetable or canola

¼ cup [12 g] chopped green onions (3 or 4 green onions)

⅓ cup [40 g] minced garlic (about 12 cloves)

¼ oz [7 g] toasted seaweed, for garnish (usually one box of packaged toasted seaweed)

1. Separate the egg yolks and whites and set the whites aside.

2. In a medium bowl, combine the cooked rice, egg yolks, chili crisp, sesame oil, oyster sauce, soy sauce, and salt. Mix until the rice is well coated.

3. In a large pan, preferably a wok, over high heat, add the neutral oil. Add half of the green onions and cook for 45 to 60 seconds, or until fragrant. Then add the minced garlic to the pan and cook for 1 minute, or until lightly brown but not burnt. Add the egg whites to the pan. Cook for 1 minute, or until the egg whites are mixed in with the aromatics and no longer wet.

4. Add the seasoned rice to the pan. Stir-fry everything for 2 to 4 minutes, or until all the rice grains are mixed in with the other ingredients. Taste and season it with more salt if necessary. Be mindful that it gets topped with slightly salty, toasted seaweed, so the rice shouldn't be too salty. Right before serving, add the rest of the chopped green onions and stir-fry everything for 30 seconds.

5. Transfer to a serving plate. Crumble the toasted seaweed on top of the rice. Serve immediately.

Chili Crisp Biscuits *with* Honey-Butter Glaze

Biscuits are personal. You can tell that people have strong opinions about what biscuits are and how they should taste by looking at the number of biscuit recipes that are out there. Some are extra flaky with layers, and others are slightly doughy. I've made many different types of biscuits, but when I tried a recipe for butter biscuits, I felt I finally found my match.

Butter biscuits, as the name suggests, start with a whole stick of butter, which gets swirled around the baking pan. The biscuit dough, which comes together quickly, gets baked in the pool of butter, creating a fantastic crunch on the bottom. The addition of salt, ground pepper, and chili crisp in the batter makes it extra flavorful, but the honey-butter glaze takes it to the next level. The sweet-and-spicy glaze gets brushed on top of the biscuits when they are done baking in the oven. The residual heat slightly melts the glaze while naturally coating the top, and it adds so much flavor to the biscuits that you truly don't need to top them with anything else. But because of their square shape, these biscuits are ideal for breakfast sandwiches. I once made a life-changing bite with fried Spam, fried hash browns, and fried eggs, all sandwiched between just-baked chili crisp biscuits, so I highly suggest you do the same! Regardless of how you define the perfect biscuit, there's no denying that these chili crisp biscuits are incredible.

MAKES 9 OR 16 BISCUITS,
DEPENDING ON THE SIZE

CHILI CRISP BISCUITS

2½ cups [350 g] all-purpose flour

1 Tbsp baking powder

2 tsp granulated sugar

2 tsp kosher salt

2 tsp freshly ground black pepper

1 tsp baking soda

1½ cups [360 ml] cold buttermilk

2 Tbsp chili crisp

½ cup [113 g] salted butter

HONEY-BUTTER GLAZE

3 Tbsp salted butter

3 Tbsp honey

1 Tbsp chili crisp

1. Preheat the oven to 400°F [200°C].

2. **To make the biscuits:** In a large bowl, add the flour, baking powder, sugar, salt, pepper, and baking soda and whisk to combine.

3. In a separate medium bowl, add the buttermilk and chili crisp and mix to combine.

4. Pour the wet mixture into the dry mixture. Using a rubber spatula, stir until a shaggy dough forms and there's no flour mixture left. Make sure not to overmix the dough.

5. In a medium sauté pan or skillet over medium-low heat, melt the butter. Pour the melted butter into a 9 in [23 cm] square baking dish and swirl it around to make sure it coats all four sides.

6. Transfer the dough to the buttered baking pan. Moisten your hands with water and press the dough evenly into the pan until it covers the whole pan. Using damp hands will prevent the dough from sticking. Let a pool of butter in the baking pan overflow on top of the dough, especially around the corners, while pressing it with your hands.

cont'd.

7. Using either a paring knife or a bench scraper, cut the dough into nine squares. You can cut it into sixteen pieces if you want smaller biscuits. Precutting the dough before baking makes portioning much easier.

8. Bake the biscuits in the preheated oven for 25 to 27 minutes, or until the top has turned golden brown and the biscuits have puffed up to fill the baking pan.

9. **To make the honey-butter glaze:** While the biscuits are baking, in a small bowl, add the butter. Microwave it for 20 to 30 seconds, or until the butter melts. Add the honey and chili crisp to the melted butter and whisk to combine. Set aside.

10. Once the biscuits are done baking, take them out of the oven. While the biscuits are still hot, using a paring knife or a bench scraper, cut along the seams of the biscuit dough to separate each portion. Let sit for about 5 minutes, so the biscuits are still warm but not piping hot.

11. Pour the honey-butter glaze over the biscuits while they're still in the baking pan. Let the glaze cool for at least 15 minutes before serving. Serve the biscuits with extra chili crisp, if desired, and with a nub of butter. The leftovers can be stored in an airtight container at room temperature for up to 3 days. Or you can freeze them for up to 1 month and reheat them in the oven at 400°F [200°C] for 10 minutes, or until they are warm and slightly crunchy on top.

Spicy Cream Cheese Dip *with* Smoked Salmon

I never considered myself a dip guy. It's just something that I never craved. But smoked salmon, on the other hand, is something that I crave all the time (I'm probably thinking about smoked salmon now). One day, I felt too lazy to layer pieces of smoked salmon on a thick smear of cream cheese (I was feeling REALLY LAZY, okay?), so I thought to myself, "Why not turn this into a dip?" And my perfect, dreamy dip was born. Whipped cream cheese and sour cream—the base for many good dips—meet savory chili crisp, transforming the white dip into a visually pleasing rosy-pink color. Nice bites of salty smoked salmon and fresh, raw green onion make this dip irresistible. Serve it with crackers, bagels, or celery sticks.

1. In a small bowl, add all the ingredients and mix together. Once everything is well combined, cover and chill in the fridge for about 30 minutes.

2. Serve cold with raw veggies, toasted bagels, potato chips, crackers, and more. The leftovers can be stored in the fridge in an airtight container for up to 3 days.

SERVES 2 TO 4

½ cup [120 g] whipped cream cheese

¼ cup [60 g] sour cream

2 Tbsp chili crisp

1 Tbsp fresh lemon juice

1 Tbsp rice wine vinegar

1 tsp lemon zest

1 tsp kosher salt

3 oz [85 g] smoked salmon, chopped

3 green onions, chopped

Raw vegetables, toasted bagels, potato chips, or crackers, for serving

Spicy Tomato *and* Egg Soup

I love having soup for breakfast. It offers the same comfort as sipping a hot cup of coffee to start a day, but with more flavors! I crave this spicy tomato and egg soup, especially as my hangover cure the morning after a night of too much drinking. When I first tasted this easy homey Chinese soup, I immediately thought of gyeran-guk, Korean egg drop soup. I tried a lot of Chinese comfort food after I moved to the United States, and it was so special to experience familiar yet different flavors each time. Regardless of my Korean identity, the comfort I felt from enjoying this soup was universal.

Taking the time to cook tomatoes in green onion and garlic–infused oil releases their sweet and tangy natural juices, creating an incredible broth with minimal seasonings. Using chili crisp early in the cooking process, rather than as a finishing touch, adds pleasant heat and umami and allows the flavors to deepen.

You can enjoy the soup on its own, but I love eating it gukbap style, which means rice served with the soup in Korean cuisine. Add a scoop of warm rice to the soup bowl and pour the soup directly on top of the rice. Or use this soup as a base for your favorite noodle soup. Starting a day with this warm, flavorful soup will make a big difference in your energy throughout the day, especially if you have a hangover. It works like magic for me every single time!

SERVES 2 OR 3

1 Tbsp neutral oil, such as vegetable or canola

4 green onions, chopped

3 garlic cloves, minced (about 1 Tbsp)

3 medium tomatoes, roughly chopped into 2 to 3 in [5 to 7.5 cm] chunks

1 tsp kosher salt, plus more as needed

¼ cup [60 g] chili crisp

½ medium yellow onion, sliced

2 cups [480 ml] chicken broth or water

1 Tbsp light soy sauce

2 tsp rice wine vinegar

1 tsp toasted sesame oil

2 tsp cornstarch

3 large eggs

Warm rice or cooked noodles, for serving

1. In a large pot over medium-high heat, heat the neutral oil. Set aside 1 Tbsp of the green parts of the chopped green onions and add the rest of the green onions and the minced garlic to the pot. Sauté for 30 to 60 seconds, or until fragrant. Add the tomato chunks and salt, and cook for 2 to 4 minutes, or until the tomatoes are softened. Add the chili crisp and sliced onion to the pot. Cook for 1 minute while stirring.

2. Add the 2 cups [480 ml] broth and bring it to a boil, then turn the heat to low, season the soup with soy sauce, rice wine vinegar, and sesame oil, and let simmer for 5 to 10 minutes.

3. While the soup is simmering, prepare a slurry by mixing the cornstarch with 1 Tbsp of water in a small bowl. Set it aside.

cont'd.

49

4. Crack the eggs into a bowl, and beat them until the whites and yolks are fully mixed, preferably using chopsticks.

5. Bring the heat to medium-high, then slowly pour the beaten eggs in a circular motion into the simmering broth. Don't touch the eggs for 2 minutes, or until the curdled eggs come up to the surface. Then gently break the eggs apart with a spoon.

6. Stir in the prepared cornstarch slurry and let it simmer for a few minutes more, or until the broth gets slightly shiny and thicker. Season with more salt if necessary.

7. Serve immediately with the reserved chopped green onions for garnish. Serve with a side of a warm rice or cooked noodles for noodle soup. The leftovers can be stored in an airtight container in the fridge for up to 4 days.

Spiced Granola

My go-to Christmas present has always been a big batch of homemade granola. It takes a little effort and experiementation to make but gives you high rewards of nutrition and flavors. And chili crisp is a perfect flavor booster to take your granola to the next level.

It may seem like a lot of chili crisp at first, but the maple syrup tames the heat while adding nutty, caramel flavors to the oats. The secret ingredient in this granola is sumac. Sumac is a popular spice in Middle Eastern cuisine. Sprinkling sumac on the oats adds a bright, citrusy flavor that comes through so pleasantly.

Just like any granola recipe out there, this is a good formula that's highly customizable. If you want to go a little easy on spices, feel free to add less. Add any types of nuts and dried fruits you like. My favorite way of enjoying this is with a nice dollop of Greek yogurt. The savory, spicy granola flavors meld with the yogurt as it mixes. It's just what I need when taking a quick break during the day.

MAKES 5 CUPS [550 G]

¼ cup [60 ml] neutral oil, such as vegetable or canola

½ cup [120 ml] maple syrup

3 Tbsp chili crisp

1 Tbsp sumac

2 tsp smoked paprika

1 tsp kosher salt

3 cups [300 g] old-fashioned rolled oats

1 cup [100 g] sliced almonds

½ cup [80 g] dried apricots, chopped

½ cup [40 g] unsweetened shredded coconut

1. Preheat the oven to 300°F [150°C]. Line a baking sheet with parchment paper.

2. In a medium bowl, whisk together the oil, maple syrup, chili crisp, sumac, paprika, and salt. Add the oats and almonds. Stir everything together so that the oats and almonds are fully coated with the seasonings.

3. Transfer the seasoned oats to the prepared baking sheet and spread into an even layer. Make sure there are some clumps of seasoned oat mixtures to create clusters.

4. Bake for 25 to 30 minutes, stirring halfway through.

5. Take it out of the oven. Add the apricots and coconut to the oats while they are still warm. Mix everything together, preferably using two spatulas. If you want to create clumps, press down a few chunks of granola pieces while it's still warm, then let it cool.

6. Cool completely. The granola can be stored in an airtight container at room temperature for up 1 month.

chapter 2

NOODLES AND CARBS

HOW CHILI CRISP HELPED ME EMBRACE MY IDENTITY IN AMERICA

When I first came to America, I was only thirteen years old. Unlike many immigrants, I didn't come here with my family; I came here alone, escorted by flight attendants because I was too young to travel alone. The moment that I walked out of the gate at the Dallas International Airport, I immediately noticed all these people from different cultures, who looked nothing like me. I was overwhelmed, not knowing where I would fit in.

I didn't know how to navigate or where I belonged as a middle school student in Austin, Texas. My English was okay, but I was insecure about it. I tried my best to make friends, but often I wouldn't understand a few phrases, and I looked them up in the dictionary that I carried with me. I started to notice that so-called popular kids didn't look like me. I felt as if there was an invisible separation between Asian students like myself in the ESL class and everyone else. That's when I unconsciously realized that if I wanted to assimilate to American culture or be a part of the popular group, I had to hide my Asian identity. Because I couldn't change how I looked, I cut out all the things that made me feel Korean. I didn't talk about my love for K-pop, Asian food, or anything. I started making more friends as I put more effort into understanding the American culture. The closer I crossed that invisible line, the further I went from my real identity.

This mindset continued after I moved to Alabama for high school. Even though there were more opportunities to be a part of the Korean and Asian communities, I constantly pushed them away. I had this false narrative that hanging out with other Asian people would keep me from being welcomed by "popular" kids. I tried my best not to talk to the few Korean students at my school. I actively didn't include them as my friend group continued to expand. I wanted to be like everyone else, so I never owned or embraced my Asianness publicly. At home, I was devouring Asian food and kimchi, but at school, I brought frozen

Lean Cuisine because that's what other people were eating. I pretended that I wasn't Asian for years.

Looking back, I was foolish to think hiding and actively denying my identity was a way to succeed in America. I know that that's no longer true, but I didn't have a vehicle to show who I was and tell people about my Asian identity.

Cultural identity was not a concept that I had to think about while growing up in Korea. I was surrounded only by other Korean people. I wasn't exposed to other cultures where I noticed anything different, visually or culturally. Living in America, a melting pot of so many wonderful cultures, I felt like my Asian-ness sometimes made me feel lesser than the majority. As I continued to work through navigating my identity, I realized there were years of denial and internal sabotage that prevented me from fully embracing who I was as a Korean immigrant in America.

This false narrative and self-sabotage started to change after I came to New York. I was exposed to diverse Asian food scenes, and I started connecting with more Asian friends through our mutual love of Asian food. I mean, having so many options for Asian groceries in New York opened my mind, eyes, taste, and curiosity to other Asian diasporas.

Casually walking into Asian grocery markets where I could see other people who looked like me, picking up things that I was too afraid to even talk about, was really empowering. After trying different Asian products and condiments beyond the Korean seasonings and staples that I knew about, I started to feel more like myself. I remember how happy and alive I felt when I tasted steamed dumplings drizzled with spicy chili crisp.

Chili crisp is a vessel for me to really connect to other Asian cultures and help me show who I am. Chili crisp isn't uniquely Korean; it's more of a symbol of universal Asian flavors. But it helped me change the false narrative that I held for years that I couldn't be friends with other Asian people to succeed in America. I thought being friends with Asian people gave me less chance of being a part of the American culture that I desperately wanted to join. Through chili crisp, I created many meaningful friendships with people who helped me embrace and celebrate my Asian identity.

Spicy, umami, slightly funky, wonderfully salty, slightly sweet, delightfully crunchy—chili crisp's flavors remind me of home; these are the flavors that I constantly crave and that make me happy.

Everyone, along with me as your chili crisp hype man, says chili crisp is universal and goes well with everything, including noodles, pasta, risotto, and more. There are no borders or boundaries as to where chili crisp can go (as you can see in many of many recipes in the book!). Its distinct flavor adds oomph to everything. It can be adapted to any dish. Its versatility speaks to me.

Chili crisp opened the door of connections with other Asian cultures for me. The more I tasted chili crisp, the more I appreciated it and was proud to be a part of it. It even became my pickup line when making new friends. Do you know about chili crisp? Do you like chili crisp? What's your favorite way of enjoying it? Do you want to try my chili crisp? I always end up having fun, delicious conversations with new friends, and I love inspiring and being inspired to hear all the creative ways that people enjoy chili crisp.

Now, as I have developed my own chili crisp, it has become a vessel to talk about my Korean identity. A lot of chili crisp that you see on the market doesn't have gochugaru, Korean red pepper flakes, in general. But because I use gochugaru in my chili crisp, it becomes Korean. It's different from other chili crisps, and it's a way to combine my Korean identity with countless other unique blends of flavors that tell their own stories.

Just like chili crisp goes with everything while adding its own flavor, I want to be adaptable while still bringing my own flair. I want to add my flavor to wherever I end up being, and I want my flavor to go with everything else. That's what chili crisp is for me. It goes with everything, and I want to be that person.

Instant Tan Tan Shin Ramyun

Tantanmen is a Japanese take on dan dan noodles, or dandanmian, a popular noodle dish in Chinese Sichuan cuisine. There are four important components in dan dan noodles: spicy chili oil, a savory meat mixture, a nutty sauce, and wheat noodles with leafy vegetables. Unlike dan dan noodles, which don't have any broth, Japanese tantanmen typically comes with a flavorful broth. Every time I sip this nutty, spicy broth, I can't help but smile and forget all my worries. It sounds cheesy, but that's the power of good broth, especially tantanmen.

This recipe is an instant way to create the spicy, nutty flavors of tantanmen. It starts with my absolute favorite brand of instant noodles, Shin Ramyun, which has addictively spicy flavors that complement chili crisp well. When assembling tantanmen, the savory meat mixture and broth are prepared separately. But in this dish, everything happens in one pot so that the broth can develop even deeper flavors. The tahini and soy milk combination adds nutty, savory flavors and creates a rich, creamy broth in minutes.

I love to dollop chili crisp on Korean instant ramyun to bring different types of heat to the broth, and this is just another delicious way to use chili crisp to level up instant ramyun. If you love things that are both spicy and creamy, this easy recipe is for you.

SERVES 2

2 large eggs

1 Tbsp neutral oil, such as vegetable or canola

1 lb [455 g] ground pork

3 green onions, chopped

3 garlic cloves, minced

2 Tbsp mirin

2 Tbsp soy sauce

Two 4.2 oz [120 g] packages Shin Ramyun or any spicy ramyun noodles, including seasoning packets (powdered seasoning and dehydrated vegetables)

1 Tbsp gochujang

1 medium yellow onion, sliced

3 Tbsp tahini

3 Tbsp chili crisp, plus more for serving

2 cups [480 ml] chicken broth (or any type of broth)

2 cups [480 ml] soy milk

3 heads baby bok choy

1. Add enough water to a large pot to submerge the eggs and bring to a boil; prepare a bowl with ice-cold water. Add the eggs to the boiling water and cook for 6½ minutes. Transfer the eggs to the prepared ice bath to shock and stop the cooking. Peel the soft-boiled eggs and set them aside.

2. In a heavy-bottom pot over medium-high heat, add the oil and cook the pork for 3 to 4 minutes, or until it's no longer pink. Set aside 1 Tbsp of the green part of the chopped green onions, add the rest to the pot with the pork, along with the garlic, and sauté for a few minutes, or until fragrant. Season the meat with the mirin, soy sauce, one entire powdered seasoning packet, and gochujang and continue to cook until most of the moisture has evaporated, 3 to 5 minutes.

3. Once the ground pork mixture is seasoned and slightly crisped, add the onion, followed by the tahini and chili crisp. Stir to combine.

cont'd.

4. Add the chicken broth and soy milk to the pot. Add only half of another powdered seasoning packet and both of the dried vegetable seasoning packets. Bring to a boil, then add the noodles and constantly lift them up and down in the boiling broth until fully cooked, about 4 minutes or the cooking time for the noodles listed on the package. After the first 2 minutes of cooking the noodles, add the bok choy.

5. Divide the noodles between two bowls and garnish with the reserved green onions, the soft-boiled eggs, and an extra drizzle of chili crisp on top. Serve immediately.

NOTES: The noodles will absorb the broth during cooking. If you want a brothier ramyun, cook the noodles separately. Then, assemble the dish by adding the cooked noodles to the bowls first, then pouring the broth on top and garnishing.

There are so many creative uses for Shin Ramyun seasoning powder. You can make this recipe again with your choice of noodles or use the seasoning packet to season your meat and veggies. You can even use it as an ingredient to make your chili crisp blend. The seasoning already has spices and flavors, which will be a great addition to chili crisp!

Korean-Style Mapo Tofu *over* Noodles

Mapo tofu is one of the first Sichuan dishes that I ever tasted. Tingling peppercorns in the sauce! Chili oil–covered tofu! Even though I was sweating profusely, I inhaled the mapo tofu. Traditionally, mapo tofu uses doubanjiang, spicy bean sauce, to create a savory, tangy broth. I wanted to create a similar flavor profile with Korean pantry staples, like gochujang and gochugaru. They bring different nuances of heat compared to Sichuan peppercorns and doubanjiang but are equally fragrant and flavorful.

What I love about this dish is the way the tofu is prepared. For traditional mapo tofu, silken tofu is mixed into the spicy, tingling sauce toward the end. But, for this recipe, firm tofu gets seared first before being incorporated into the sauce. Even after being mixed into the sauce, the crispy tofu can stand on its own and adds a nice texture.

You can serve this with rice, but I particularly enjoy eating mapo tofu with wheat noodles, specifically swirly Taiwanese sliced noodles. The sauce clings beautifully to the noodles' wavy edges, and you get a different type of pleasure compared to eating mapo tofu with rice. When I feel frisky, I sometimes enjoy this mapo tofu sauce with noodles first, followed by scoops of rice to soak up all the sauce. Double carbs to enjoy this flavorful, spicy sauce? That's my way of eating my feelings.

SERVES 2 TO 4

1 lb [455 g] firm tofu, drained

2 tsp kosher salt

1 tsp freshly ground black pepper

2 Tbsp neutral oil, such as vegetable or canola

4 green onions, chopped

3 garlic cloves, minced (about 1 Tbsp)

1 Tbsp minced ginger

1 lb [455 g] ground pork (or beef)

1 medium yellow onion, diced

2 Tbsp gochujang

2 Tbsp oyster sauce

2 Tbsp soy sauce

1 Tbsp gochugaru

1/3 cup [70 g] chili crisp

1 1/2 cups [360 ml] chicken broth

1 Tbsp potato starch (or cornstarch)

1 tsp toasted sesame oil

1 tsp black vinegar

3 1/2 oz [100 g] dry wheat noodles (Taiwanese sliced noodles, such as Guan Miao sliced noodles)

1. Squeeze out extra moisture from the tofu by pressing it between paper towels or a dish towel. Cut it into 1 in [2.5 cm] cubes. Season it with 1 tsp of the salt and ½ tsp of the pepper.

2. In a large skillet, sauté pan, or wok over medium-high heat, add 1 Tbsp of the neutral oil. Add the tofu and pan-fry on all sides for 3 to 4 minutes total, or until light golden brown. Depending on the size of the pan, do this step in batches to make sure not to crowd the pan. Set the tofu aside once done pan-frying.

3. In the same pan, heat the remaining 1 Tbsp of oil over medium-high heat. Set aside 1 Tbsp of the green parts of the chopped green onion for garnish, then add the rest of the green onions, garlic, and ginger to the pan, and sauté for 1 minute, or until fragrant.

cont'd.

4. Add the pork to the pan and season it with the remaining 1 tsp of salt and ½ tsp of pepper. Break the meat apart into small pieces using a wooden spoon or a spatula. Add the diced onion and continue to cook for 2 to 3 minutes, or until the ground meat is no longer pink and the onion looks slightly translucent.

5. Meanwhile, in a small bowl, add the gochujang, oyster sauce, soy sauce, gochugaru, and chili crisp and stir to combine. Once it's become a homogeneous seasoning paste, add it to the ground meat mixture and sauté for 2 to 3 minutes more, or until the ground meat fully absorbs all the seasonings, then add the chicken broth.

6. Bring the mixture to a boil and then simmer for 5 to 7 more minutes to develop the flavors. Then, add the fried tofu cubes to the sauce and cook for a few more minutes, or until the fried tofu cubes absorb some broth.

7. Meanwhile, make a slurry by mixing the potato starch with 1 Tbsp of water. Gradually add the slurry to the sauce to get the desired consistency, adding more as needed. If it gets too thick, add more water.

8. Finish the mapo tofu sauce by adding the toasted sesame oil and black vinegar.

9. Cook the wheat noodles according to the package directions. Assemble the dish by dividing the cooked noodles among bowls, ladling a generous amount of the mapo tofu sauce on top, and garnishing with an extra spoonful of chili crisp and the reserved green onions. The leftovers can be stored in an airtight container in the fridge for 2 to 3 days.

Bibim Guksu *with* Cucumber, Green Onions, *and* Jammy Eggs

Bibim guksu is a cold Korean noodle dish that takes only a few minutes. *Bibim* means "mixed" and *guksu* means "noodles" in Korean, so it translates as "mixed noodles." Typically, it's made with a mix of gochujang and sour, fermented kimchi and lots of toasted sesame oil, all tossed with cooked somen noodles. It's a refreshing dish that I particularly enjoy slurping during summer.

One of my favorite things about making bibim guksu is mixing noodles with the sauce. It's called son-mat in Korean, which translates to "hand taste." You have to use your hands to mix the noodles with the sauce. It's a different experience from just mixing noodles with tongs or chopsticks!

My mom used to make this for me during the summer when I didn't have much appetite. She would add scoops of gochujang, soy sauce, and toasted sesame oil without any measurement to a big bowl. Then, she would mix the noodles with the sauce aggressively with her clean hands, wrap the noodles around them, and feed me straight into my mouth. And magically, all my appetite would come back, and she and I would quickly finish a ridiculous amount of noodles together.

For this recipe, instead of leaning into gochujang, I use the savory, spicy flavors of chili crisp as the main ingredient. The salty, vinegary, and sweet flavors create a mouthwatering sauce. It has a nostalgic taste yet feels different from what I grew up eating. It has become my go-to noodle dish when I want to quickly whip up something flavorful. Be sure to add sliced Persian cucumber for a refreshing crunch!

2 large eggs

2 to 3 Tbsp chili crisp

2 Tbsp soy sauce

1 ½ tsp rice wine vinegar

1 Tbsp toasted sesame oil, plus more for drizzling

1 Tbsp granulated sugar

3 garlic cloves, minced (about 1 Tbsp)

2 green onions, chopped

3½ oz [100 g] noodles, preferably somen

½ medium yellow onion, sliced

1 Tbsp toasted sesame seeds

1 Persian cucumber, julienned

1. Add enough water to a large pot to submerge the eggs and bring to a boil; fill a bowl with ice-cold water. Once the water starts to boil, add the eggs and cook for 6½ minutes. Transfer the eggs to the prepared ice bath and set aside.

2. In a large bowl, add the chili crisp, soy sauce, rice wine vinegar, sesame oil, sugar, and garlic. Reserve about 1 Tbsp of the green parts of the chopped green onions for garnish, add the remaining green onions to the bowl, and whisk everything to combine.

3. Cook a bundle of noodles according to the package directions. Add the sliced onion to the pot and cook with the noodles for 1 minute. Drain the noodles and onions in a colander and rinse under cold water to eliminate any extra starch. Squeeze the noodles as hard as possible to remove excess moisture before mixing them with the sauce.

4. Add the cooked noodles to the large bowl of seasonings. Add the sesame seeds. Preferably using hands with gloves on, mix the noodles with everything else.

5. Peel the reserved soft-boiled eggs. Transfer the mixed, cold noodles to a serving plate. Garnish with the reserved green onions, peeled soft-boiled eggs, and sliced Persian cucumber. Drizzle with about 1 tsp toasted sesame oil right before serving.

Spicy Miso Butter Linguini *with* Mushrooms

When I first tried this pantry-friendly pasta, my eyes opened wide after the first slurp. The combination of umami-packed ingredients like miso, chili crisp, and oyster sauce creates a wonderful balance of salty and spicy flavors. A variety of mushrooms adds a nice, meaty texture to this savory pasta. Linguine is a perfect shape to absorb the flavorful sauce, but any noodle-like pasta, such as spaghetti or fettuccine, will work great in this dish.

The best part of eating this pasta is breaking the luscious egg yolk and mixing it with the pasta. Even though it's a garnish, it adds an important layer of creamy, rich flavor to the pasta, so don't skip it! The residual heat of the pasta turns the egg yolk into a delicious cream sauce, similar to carbonara.

SERVES 6 TO 8

2 lb [910 g] fresh mushrooms, such as cremini, shiitake, oyster, or a combination (see Note)

10 Tbsp neutral oil, such as vegetable or canola, for frying

Kosher salt

Freshly ground black pepper

1 lb [455 g] linguine pasta

⅓ cup [70 g] chili crisp

¼ cup [60 g] miso

2 Tbsp light soy sauce

2 Tbsp rice wine vinegar

1 Tbsp oyster sauce

1½ tsp sesame oil

¼ cup [55 g] unsalted butter

3 garlic cloves, minced (about 1 Tbsp)

Freshly grated Parmesan cheese, for garnish

6 to 8 large egg yolks, for garnish

1. Clean the mushrooms with a damp paper towel to get rid of any dirt. Cut the mushrooms into bite-size pieces. If you use cremini or shiitake, remove the stems and slice them into ¼ in [6 mm] thick pieces. If you use oyster mushrooms, shred them into pieces with your hands.

2. In a large skillet or sauté pan, preferably cast iron, heat 3 Tbsp of the oil over medium-high heat. Add one-third of the mushrooms, spreading them in an even layer, and cook for about 5 minutes or until deeply browned on the bottom. Transfer the mushrooms to a plate, and repeat with the remaining mushrooms, cooking with 3 Tbsp of oil per batch. Be sure not to overseason your mushrooms, because they get tossed with the seasonings later. Wipe out the pan.

3. Meanwhile, cook the linguine according to the package directions, until al dente. Reserve ½ cup [120 ml] of the pasta water, then drain.

4. In a small bowl, whisk together the the chili crisp, miso, light soy sauce, rice wine vinegar, oyster sauce, and sesame oil. Set the sauce aside.

5. In the same pan, melt the butter over medium-high heat. Once the butter is melted and starts to brown slightly, add the garlic and cook for 1 minute, or until fragrant.

6. Add the drained linguine to the pan. Pour the reserved sauce along with the reserved cooked mushrooms to the cooked pasta and toss everything over low heat. Use the reserved pasta water, as needed, to coat the noodles with sauce until they look glossy.

7. When ready to serve, divide the pasta into bowls and top it with the Parmesan and 1 egg yolk per serving. Serve immediately. The leftovers can be stored in an airtight container in the fridge for up to 5 days.

NOTE: I highly recommend having a blend of assorted mushrooms for different textures, but if you choose just one kind, go with shiitake mushrooms.

Chili Crisp Bucatini Carbonara

As an egg yolk lover, I adore carbonara. The rich yolky sauce that coats the noodles is truly magical! But, whenever I enjoy carbonara, I crave something sharp, spicy, and vinegary to balance the rich sauce. After devouring a rich carbonara dish, I would open my tub of kimchi and eat straight out of the jar, standing in front of my fridge.

But how about incorporating spice into the carbonara sauce? The addition of chili crisp turns the rich yolk sauce a beautiful amber-orange. When you slurp the pasta, it goes from being rich and luscious to peppery and spicy, then sharp and salty thanks to the Parmesan. It's an endlessly delicious cycle of flavors!

You can substitute bacon instead of pancetta, but pancetta has more distinct porky flavors that make the sauce worthy of devouring. And the egg yolk at the end creates a stunning presentation and a decadent sauce. Feel and taste the joy and excitement of breaking the yolk with this spicy, flavorful, and yolky carbonara!

SERVES 3 OR 4

4 oz [115 g] pancetta, cut into small cubes

3 large egg yolks, plus 1 large egg yolk per serving

1 cup [100 g] grated Parmesan cheese, plus more for garnish

3 Tbps chili crisp

8 oz [230 g] bucatini

1 tsp freshly ground black pepper

1. In a large skillet or sauté pan over medium-low heat, render the fat from the pancetta until it gets crispy, about 5 minutes. Transfer to a plate and set aside. Strain the rendered pork fat through a fine-mesh sieve into a small bowl and set aside.

2. In a large bowl, whisk together the 3 egg yolks, Parmesan cheese, chili crisp, and 1 Tbsp of the reserved pork fat.

3. Meanwhile, cook the bucatini according to the package directions, until al dente. Reserve ½ cup [120 ml] of pasta water, then drain.

4. Add the drained pasta to the egg yolk mixture and gradually add about 2 Tbsp of the pasta water while constantly tossing with tongs. Add the pepper and crispy pancetta and continue to toss until the sauce coats the pasta and thickens.

5. When ready to serve, divide the noodles among bowls and garnish with more freshly grated Parmesan cheese and an egg yolk on top of each portion.

Fiery Spaghetti *and* Meatballs

One of the first "fun" chili crisp pairings I experimented with was to add a few dollops on top of spaghetti tossed with simple marinara sauce. The tangy, slightly sweet tomato flavors from the marinara sauce felt complete with spice. And that got me thinking, Why add chili crisp only as a final garnish? Why not incorporate it as seasoning when making tomato sauce? That's how I came up with this recipe, a spicy twin of classic spaghetti and meatballs. The meatballs have gochujang to emphasize the chili crisp's flavors, and soy sauce adds more umami taste. You can cook these meatballs without making the marinara sauce if you want, but cooking them in tangy tomato sauce makes the balls more flavorful, tender, and juicy.

Despite the large amount of chili crisp used in the recipe, you won't find this dish overly spicy. There are many bold flavors, like meat and tomato, that can handle the spice. The subtle heat of the chili crisp in both the meatballs and the sauce makes this dish highly satisfying and adds a deeper flavor than if you were to use chili crisp only as a topping. Of course you should still dollop more chili crisp on top!

1. **To make the meatballs:** Let the ground meat come to room temperature first. Then, in a mixing bowl, mix together the chili crisp, gochujang, and soy sauce to combine. Add the ground beef, ground pork, mozzarella, Parmesan, panko, basil, green onions, eggs, soy sauce, gochujang, salt, and pepper. Mix everything to combine, preferably with gloves or clean hands.

2. Portion the meatball mixture into ⅓ cup [80 g] or ½ cup [120 g] balls. Put them on a baking sheet. Set aside.

3. In a large, heavy-bottom pot, such as a Dutch oven, over medium-high heat, add about ¼ in [6 mm] of oil, and working in batches, sear the prepared meatballs on all sides until they are golden brown, 3 to 5 minutes. Set aside. Discard any excess oil.

SERVES 6 TO 8

MEATBALLS

1½ lb [680 g] ground beef (75% lean)

1 lb [455 g] ground pork

¼ cup [60 g] chili crisp

3 Tbsp gochujang

2 Tbsp soy sauce

½ cup [40 g] shredded mozzarella cheese

½ cup [50 g] grated Parmesan cheese, plus more for garnish

½ cup [30 g] panko

½ cup [6 g] loosely packed fresh basil, chopped, plus more for garnish

4 green onions, chopped

2 large eggs

2 Tbsp soy sauce

3 Tbsp gochujang

1 tsp kosher salt

½ tsp freshly ground black pepper

Olive oil, for frying

4. **To make the marinara sauce with spaghetti:** Pour the canned whole peeled tomatoes into a large bowl. Using your hands or a wooden spoon, break apart the tomatoes into pieces. You can use canned crushed tomatoes instead, but this method will create more textures and flavors in the sauce. Add 1 cup [240 ml] of water to the tomatoes.

5. In the same pot that you cooked the meatballs in over medium-high heat, add the olive oil and sliced garlic and cook for 30 seconds, or until fragrant. Don't let it brown. Once fragrant, add the tomato paste and chili crisp and cook for 1 minute, or until the tomato paste gets slightly caramelized. Add the tomatoes to the pot while scraping up any brown bits from the bottom. Season with the sugar and soy sauce.

6. Add the prepared seared meatballs to the tomato sauce.

Cover and let simmer over low heat, stirring occasionally, for 45 to 50 minutes, or until the sauce is slightly reduced and the meatballs are coated in the sauce.

7. Meanwhile, cook the spaghetti according to the package directions, until al dente. Reserve ½ cup [120 ml] of the pasta water, then drain.

8. When ready to serve, spoon the marinara sauce over the cooked spaghetti and toss with a little bit of reserved pasta water until all the noodles are coated with the sauce. Divide the tossed spaghetti into bowls and add the meatballs on top. Garnish with a spoonful of extra marinara sauce, freshly grated Parmesan cheese, and chopped basil. The leftover sauce can be stored in an airtight container in the fridge for up to 5 days.

MARINARA SAUCE WITH SPAGHETTI

Two 28 oz [795 g] cans whole peeled tomatoes or crushed tomatoes

¼ cup [60 ml] extra-virgin olive oil

5 garlic cloves, thinly sliced

6 oz [170 g] tomato paste

⅓ cup [70 g] chili crisp

1 Tbsp granulated sugar

1½ tsp soy sauce

1 lb [455 g] spaghetti

Creamy Rigatoni *with* Crispy Chickpeas, Spinach, *and* Lemony Panko

Chili crisp is often associated only with Asian dishes, like dumplings and noodles, but it's also incredible with pasta dishes both as a finishing touch and as a sauce. A combination of heavy cream and chicken broth creates a delicious foundation for spicy chili crisp, resulting in a layered, savory sauce—without being overly spicy. Lightly crisped chickpeas and tender chicken thighs make the dish even more satisfying and hearty. The unsung hero of the dish is the bright lemon flavors in both the cream sauce and the crispy panko. I adore this weeknight-friendly pasta, and it's perfect when I want something comforting that will also make me sweat from the spice.

SERVES 2 TO 4

3 Tbsp salted butter

3 Tbsp olive oil

One 15 oz [425 g] can chickpeas, rinsed and drained

2 tsp kosher salt

1 tsp freshly ground pepper

1 medium yellow onion, sliced

1 lb [455 g] boneless chicken thighs, cut into bite-size pieces

3 Tbsp chili crisp, plus more for serving

1 cup [240 ml] chicken broth

1 cup [240 ml] heavy cream (see Note)

2 lemons

1 cup [60 g] panko

8 oz [230 g] rigatoni or any tubular pasta

5 oz [140 g] baby spinach (see Note)

1. In a heavy-bottom pot or Dutch oven over medium heat, melt 1 Tbsp of the butter with 1 Tbsp of the olive oil. Add the drained chickpeas and season them with 1 tsp of the salt and ½ tsp of the pepper. Lightly fry the chickpeas until they start to caramelize and get slightly crispy around the edges with golden-brown spots, 5 to 7 minutes. Using a slotted spoon, transfer the chickpeas to a bowl.

2. In the same pot, melt the remaining 2 Tbsp of butter over medium-high heat. Add the sliced onion and cook until it's translucent, 2 to 3 minutes. Add the chicken, season it with the remaining salt and pepper, and cook for 3 to 5 minutes. There's no need to thoroughly cook the chicken in this step because it will be cooked through in simmering broth later. Once the meat starts picking up some color, add the chili crisp and stir.

3. Once the chicken and onion are fully coated with chili crisp, add the broth and heavy cream and bring to a boil. Zest both lemons and set the zest aside. Cut one lemon and squeeze one half directly over the pot while catching any seeds. Add half of the reserved cooked chickpeas to the pot. Let it simmer while stirring for 8 to 10 minutes, or until the sauce starts to thicken slightly and the chicken is fully cooked. Slightly mash the chickpeas during this process to thicken the sauce.

cont'd.

4. In a medium sauté pan or skillet over medium heat, add the remaining 2 Tbsp of olive oil and the panko. Stir for 2 to 3 minutes, or until the panko starts to turn golden brown. Add the juice of the remaining 3 lemon halves. Keep stirring to cook off any moisture from the lemon juice, and turn off the heat when the panko gets crispy and golden brown. Stir in the reserved lemon zest and set aside.

5. In a separate pot, cook the pasta according to the package directions, but 3 minutes short of the cooking time, then transfer the al dente pasta to the pot with the simmering sauce to finish cooking. Constantly stir the pasta until thick. Season with more salt if necessary.

6. Turn off the heat and add the spinach and the remaining chickpeas to the pot. Keep stirring until the spinach is wilted.

7. Serve immediately with generous sprinkles of lemony panko and an extra drizzle of chili crisp.

NOTE: You can substitute heavy cream with regular milk or even plant-based milk. Instead of spinach, any hearty greens, such as chards, kale, or bok choy, would be great in this recipe.

Baked Chili Crisp Farfalle Pasta *with* Goat Brie Cheese

If there's one pasta that gave me a confidence boost, it's this creamy baked pasta dish made with goat Brie cheese. I picked up goat Brie cheese without any plan, and after keeping it in the back of my fridge for a while, I finally decided to make something with it. I landed on a "mac-and-cheese" idea, incorporating that slightly funky goat cheese flavor in my cheese sauce. It was different from the creamy, Cheddar cheese–heavy, orange-hued mac and cheese that I'm used to, but that distinct tang from the goat cheese was delightful. Ever since that happy Brie experiment, I've been making this pasta as my proud signature dish, fueled by many friends' praise.

Inspired by those flavors, this baked pasta goes one step further with chili crisp. The subtly smoky, spicy flavors of hot Italian sausage nicely complement the heat of chili crisp. Dried apricots get caramelized, bringing jammy sweetness to each bite, while panko at the end adds a much-needed crisp texture. You can add any cheese, but the rich, nutty flavors of Gruyère balance tangy goat Brie the best, in my opinion. The pasta isn't complete without the final drizzle of honey, which integrates all the different flavor notes into one incredibly satisfying bite.

1. Preheat the oven to 375°F [190°C] and grease a 9 by 13 in [23 by 33 cm] baking dish with butter or nonstick oil spray.

2. In a large skillet or sauté pan over medium-high heat, add a splash of olive oil. Add the sausage to the pan and break apart using the back of a wooden spoon. Sear until browned throughout, 3 to 5 minutes. Once the sausage is crisped and brown, add the onion and apricots. Sauté for 2 to 3 minutes, or until the apricots start to caramelize slightly. Season the mixture with 2 Tbsp of the chili crisp and sauté for a few minutes, or until everything is coated with chili crisp. Once the meat mixture is done, transfer it to the prepared baking dish and set aside.

cont'd.

Olive oil, for sautéing

1 lb [455 g] hot Italian sausage, casings removed

1 medium yellow onion, finely diced

½ cup [80 g] dried apricots, finely diced

4 Tbsp [60 g] chili crisp

1 lb [455 g] farfalle pasta

¼ cup [55 g] unsalted butter

¼ cup [35 g] all-purpose flour

2½ cups [600 ml] whole milk

6½ oz [185 g] goat Brie cheese, preferably Woolrich Dairy soft-ripened Triple Crème goat Brie cheese, cut into small pieces (see Note)

1 cup [100 g] shredded Gruyère cheese

1 tsp kosher salt

½ tsp freshly ground pepper

1 cup [60 g] panko

Chopped fresh parsley for garnish

Honey for drizzling

3. Meanwhile, cook the farfalle according to the package directions, until al dente. Reserve ½ cup [120 ml] of the pasta water, then drain.

4. Wipe out the pan with a paper towel to get rid of excess grease, then add the butter over medium-low heat. When the butter has melted, sprinkle in the flour to make a roux and cook until it becomes a paste, 4 to 5 minutes. Whisk in the milk until the sauce thickens, 5 to 6 minutes, or until the sauce coats the back of the spoon. Add the goat Brie and ½ cup [50 g] of the Gruyère and stir to combine. Season with the salt, pepper, and remaining 2 Tbsp of chili crisp. Continue to stir until the sauce is cheesy and cohesive. Pour the sauce over the sausage mixture in the baking dish. Mix to combine.

5. Add the steaming drained pasta directly to the baking dish with the sauce and cooked sausage mixture. Using two spatulas, mix everything until the pasta is well coated. If it's too thick, use the reserved pasta water to help coat the cooked pasta with the sauce. Spread the mixture into an even layer.

6. Sprinkle the remaining ½ cup [50 g] of Gruyère and the panko evenly over the dish.

7. Bake the pasta for 40 to 45 minutes, or until the panko has nicely browned.

Let cool for a few minutes before serving.

8. When ready to serve, divide into bowls and garnish with parsley and a drizzle of honey on top. The leftovers can be stored in an airtight container in the fridge for 3 to 5 days.

NOTE: You should be able to find goat Brie cheese at well-curated, specialty cheese shops, including at Whole Foods. If it's hard to source goat Brie cheese, you can replace it with regular Brie, but it will be missing the signature, tangy flavor that goat milk has.

Beef Short Ribs Ragù *with* Cavatappi

Short ribs are relatively expensive compared to other cuts of meat. But they are worth every penny for those luxurious nights that you want to treat yourself. They can be tough when they are not cooked properly, but when they are braised slowly for hours, their muscles break down and they become fall-apart, melt-in-your-mouth tender. Be sure to brown the short ribs on all sides to build a deep, beefy flavor foundation.

Red pepper flakes bring another layer of heat on top of spicy and umami chili crisp. Smoked paprika adds rich, smoky flavors to the ragù, while Dijon mustard brings a little bit of tang. Thanks to all these different ingredients that build on each other's flavors, the ragù sauce is decadent without being too rich and tastes like a delicious reward, especially when mixed with pasta.

1. Preheat the oven to 325°F [160° C].

2. In a deep ovenproof skillet or Dutch oven, heat the oil over medium-high heat. Generously season the short ribs with the salt and pepper.

3. Working in batches, sear the short ribs on all sides until they are deeply browned all over, 3 to 4 minutes per side. Make sure not to overcrowd the pan to ensure nice browning on all sides, then set aside. Reserve about 2 Tbsp of the fat left in the pan and discard the rest.

4. In the same pan over medium-low heat, sauté the celery, carrots, and onion for 3 to 5 minutes, or until soft. Add the garlic and cook for 1 minute more. Once fragrant, add the chili crisp, tomato paste, paprika, red pepper flakes, and mustard and sauté for a few minutes, or until the spices bloom and the tomato paste gets slightly caramelized.

5. Sprinkle in the flour, stir well, and cook for 1 minute.

6. Pour the beef stock, red wine, soy sauce, and balsamic vinegar into the pan and bring to a boil. Turn the heat to low and simmer, then return the browned short ribs to the pan, mostly submerging in the sauce.

7. Bake the short ribs in the oven for 3 hours, stirring every hour. The meat should fall off the bones and be tender when shredded.

cont'd.

SERVES 6 TO 8

2 Tbsp neutral oil, such as vegetable or canola

3 lb [1.4 kg] bone-in short ribs

1 Tbsp kosher salt

1 ½ tsp freshly ground black pepper

4 celery stalks, diced

2 medium carrots, diced

1 medium yellow onion, diced

4 garlic cloves, minced

⅓ cup [70 g] chili crisp

3 Tbsp tomato paste

1 Tbsp smoked paprika

1 ½ tsp red pepper flakes

1 ½ tsp Dijon mustard

2 Tbsp flour

1 cup [240 ml] beef stock

1 cup [240 ml] red wine

2 Tbsp soy sauce

1 Tbsp balsamic vinegar

1 lb [455 g] cavatappi pasta

Freshly grated Parmesan cheese, for garnish

Chopped fresh parsley, for garnish

8. Take the pan out of the oven and put it back on the stove over low heat to continue simmering. Remove the short ribs, shred them using two forks or tongs, and put the shredded meat back into the sauce. Let simmer for a few minutes until slightly thickened.

9. Meanwhile, cook the cavatappi according to the package directions, until al dente. Reserve ½ cup [120 ml] of the pasta water, then drain.

10. Toss the cooked noodles with the short ribs and ragù. Add some pasta water to the sauce to coat the noodles.

11. Serve immediately, garnished with Parmesan and parsley. The leftovers can be stored in an airtight container in the fridge for up to 3 days.

Spicy Pork Mandu *with* Kimchi, Tofu, *and* Glass Noodles

When people think of what foods to pair with chili crisp, dumplings might be the first food group. The spicy, umami, and salty flavors of chili crisp are the perfect touch to take dumplings to the next level. After all, dousing juicy, steamed dumplings in spicy chili oil is one of my favorite ways to eat my happy feelings! But, let's reverse-engineer this delicious formula by incorporating chili crisp as a part of the dumpling filling seasoning. By doing so, all the lovely flavors of chili crisp come through even more pleasantly.

I genuinely believe that there are no rules when it comes to dumplings. If you love juicy, meaty dumplings, go heavy on meat. If you want them to be vegetable-focused, you can add only vegetables, without any meat. It's all about your personal preferences. When it comes to my ideal dumplings, I love a variety of textures and flavors, so the more ingredients in the fillings, the better!

My fillings are inspired by mandu, Korean dumplings. Unlike other dumplings like gyoza and wontons, mandu always has these two ingredients: tofu and glass noodles, the so-called dang-myun. They make the filling tender while also adding more texture. Whether steamed or pan-fried, these dumplings are so flavorful on their own even without dipping sauce.

One of my favorite things to do is to throw dumpling parties. My friends and I come together and make dumplings while gossiping and catching up on our lives. Then, the best part is that we get to have a homemade dumpling feast after working hard together. And we all take home leftovers. Call your friends to start a new tradition of hosting dumpling parties with this recipe. Maybe make chili crisp to go with it? I will join you in spirit.

1. **To make the dumplings:** Drain the kimchi and add to a large bowl. If the kimchi isn't sour enough, add about 1 Tbsp of the vinegar.

2. Bring a large pot of water to a boil. Add the soaked, softened glass noodles and cook according to the package directions. Drain and add them

cont'd.

DUMPLINGS

1 cup [300 g] napa cabbage kimchi, preferably well fermented, cut into small pieces

1 Tbsp rice wine vinegar or apple cider vinegar (optional)

1 cup [120 g] dried glass noodles, soaked in water

8 oz [230 g] firm tofu

1 lb [455 g] ground pork

¾ cup [36 g] chopped green onions

9 garlic cloves, minced (about 3 Tbsp)

1 Tbsp minced ginger

½ cup [120 g] chili crisp

3 Tbsp soy sauce

1 Tbsp toasted sesame oil

1½ tsp rice wine vinegar

2 tsp kosher salt

1 tsp freshly ground black pepper

Two 50-wrapper packs 3½ in [9 cm] frozen round wheat dumpling wrappers, thawed in the refrigerator

2 Tbsp neutral oil, such as vegetable or canola, for frying (optional)

cont'd.

to the bowl with the kimchi. Using scissors, cut the noodles and kimchi into small pieces— they should be similar in size.

3. Squeeze the excess moisture from the tofu by twisting it in a clean kitchen towel. Squeeze and crumble the tofu into pieces similar to the texture of ground meat and add it to the bowl with kimchi and noodles. Add the pork, green onions, garlic, ginger, chili crisp, soy sauce, sesame oil, rice wine vinegar, salt, and pepper. Preferably using clean hands, or hands with gloves on, combine the mixture thoroughly.

4. Line a baking sheet with parchment paper and set up a small bowl of water next to your assembly station.

5. Place a dumpling wrapper on the palm of your hand. Dip your fingertips in the bowl of water and wet the edges of the wrapper.

6. Using a spoon or Tbsp measure, scoop about 1 Tbsp of filling onto the center of the wrapper. As long as the filling stays inside the wrapper, there's no one way of sealing a dumpling. Feel free to play around with different dumpling shapes for fun. Here are two go-to methods.

7. For half-moon-shaped pleating, wet the upper half of the dumpling wrapper and fold the dumpling wrapper in half, pinching the center tip of the dumpling edges together to seal. Using your thumb and index finger, create pleats to seal the dumpling, starting from the center and working your way to the ends of each side of the dumpling. There should be three or four pleats on each side.

8. For round pleating, wet the upper half of the dumpling wrapper, fold, and seal the dumpling completely. Wet the ends of two sides. Then, push in the middle of the sealed dumpling and bend the dumpling while connecting the two ends. Pinch them tightly to make sure the dumpling holds its shape.

9. Once the dumplings are shaped, set them on the prepared baking sheet and cover with a towel to prevent them from drying out.

10. When ready to cook the dumplings, you can either pan-fry, steam, or boil them. To pan-fry, heat the oil in a skillet or sauté pan over medium-high heat. Arrange the dumplings in an even layer and cook for 2 to 3 minutes, or until the bottoms turn golden brown. Then, bring the heat to low, add about ¼ cup [60 ml] of water to the pan, cover, and cook for 5 to 8 minutes, or until the water has evaporated and the dumpling wrappers look cooked. To steam, add an even layer of dumplings to a steamer and steam for 8 to 10 minutes, or

DIPPING SAUCE

2 garlic cloves, minced

1 green onion, chopped (both greens and whites)

2 Tbsp soy sauce

1 Tbsp chili crisp

1 Tbsp rice wine vinegar or black vinegar

1 tsp toasted sesame oil

1 tsp granulated sugar

until the dumpling wrappers look wrinkled and the fillings are slightly visible through the cooked wrapper. To boil, add the dumplings to boiling water and cook for 6 to 8 minutes, or until the dumpling wrappers look slightly puffed up and transparent.

11. **To make the dipping sauce:** In a small bowl, whisk together the garlic, green onion, soy sauce, chili crisp, vinegar, sesame oil, and sugar to combine.

12. Serve the dumplings with the dipping sauce.

13. Spread the uncooked dumplings on parchment paper–lined baking sheets so they are not touching and freeze for several hours before transferring to freezer-safe bags and freezing for up to 3 months.

Chili Crisp Tteokbokki (Spicy Rice Cakes)

Tteokbokki, plump rice cakes simmered in spicy broth, is one of my favorite Korean dishes. The sound and appearance of chewy rice cakes and fish cakes, simmering in ruby-red, sweet-and-spicy broth, makes me so happy. Theoretically, the most basic version of tteokbokki has only a few ingredients: gochujang, gochugaru, soy sauce, and sugar, along with rice and fish cakes.

Nowadays, the boundaries of what tteokbokki can be are constantly challenged with more creative, wild options. Rosé tteokbokki, one of the most beloved versions, especially in Korea, leans into a creamy sauce to balance the spice. Jjajang tteokbokki, on the other hand, uses jjajang, black bean sauce, instead of gochujang. It's time to introduce another type of tteokbokki to this ever-changing conversation: chili crisp tteokbokki.

Chili crisp adds its unique, umami-packed spice to the sauce on top of gochujang and gochugaru. And, compared to the traditional method of cooking tteok (rice cakes) in the broth, it gets lightly sautéed in chili crisp–infused oil for a boost of flavors. I personally love adding Vienna sausages (preferably made with pork) and cabbage to my tteokbokki because it makes the broth so savory. You can explore different options, like Spam or even chorizo(!), but adding some sort of meat and veggies to tteokbokki makes the sauce very flavorful. Still, no matter how you customize, be sure to add lots of green onions.

The final drizzle of heavy cream will make the sauce creamier, but it won't turn it into full rosé tteokbokki. If you want to enjoy more cream-based tteokbokki, similar to rosé tteokbokki, add milk instead of water.

SERVES 4 TO 6

3 large eggs

6 green onions

⅓ cup [70 g] chili crisp, plus more for garnish

¼ cup [60 g] applesauce

3 Tbsp gochujang

3 Tbsp light soy sauce

3 Tbsp granulated sugar

2 Tbsp gochugaru

4 garlic cloves, minced

2½ cups [500 g] rice cakes (tteok), preferably frozen wheat, but refrigerated rice flour cakes also work (see Note)

6 oz [170 g] Vienna sausages

5 sheets [275 g] squared fish cakes, cut into triangles

2 cups [170 g] chopped cabbage

½ cup [120 ml] heavy cream, plus an extra drizzle for garnish

1. In a large pot, add enough water to submerge the eggs and bring to a boil. Prepare a bowl with ice-cold water. Add the eggs to the boiling water and cook for 9 minutes. Transfer the eggs to the prepared ice bath to shock and stop the cooking. Let cool, then peel the eggs while partially submerging them in the water and set them aside.

2. Chop 1 of the green onions and set aside for garnish. Chop each of the remaining green onions crosswise into 4 pieces. Cut the thicker white parts crosswise in half.

cont'd.

3. In a small bowl, mix together the chili crisp, applesauce, gochujang, light soy sauce, sugar, gochugaru, and garlic. Set the seasoning paste aside.

4. Quickly rinse the rice cakes under water to separate them. Give the sausages a few shallow, diagonal slits. This will help make the sausages visually more pleasing and better infuse its flavors into the broth.

5. In a heavy-bottom pot over medium-high heat, add 2½ cups [600 ml] of water (or milk; see Headnote). Add the prepared seasoning paste, followed by the cut-up fish cakes, chunks of green onion, cabbage, and sausages. Bring it to a boil and simmer for 5 to 6 minutes, or until the cabbage is lightly cooked and tender. Then, add the rinsed rice cakes to the pot and cook for 3 to 5 minutes, or until they are tender to the bite. Toward the end of cooking, add the heavy cream and continue to simmer, stirring constantly, for 2 to 3 minutes, or until the cream is fully incorporated into the sauce.

6. When ready to serve, cut the cooked eggs in half. Garnish with the reserved chopped green onions, cut-up cooked eggs, and a nice drizzle of heavy cream on top, if desired. The leftovers can be stored in an airtight container in the fridge for up to 3 days.

NOTE: When it comes to choosing rice cakes, there are two kinds: rice flour-based, so-called ssal-tteok, and wheat flour-based, mil-tteok. The ones you find in the refrigerator, sometimes specifically labeled for making tteokbokki, are usually made with rice flour. They still create that nice, bouncy texture after absorbing the sauce. But, if you can, I highly recommend trying mil-tteok. It's chewier and holds its shape and texture regardless of how long it gets cooked and reheated. Mil-tteok can usually be found in the freezer section.

If you want to take this tteokbokki to the next level, pour melted mozzarella cheese on top. The extra cheese topping will tame the spice from the sauce.

Zesty Chili Crisp Focaccia

Baking is not my forte. I don't feel confident in my baking skills at all. Even when making sourdough loaves was the hobby that everyone picked up, I never followed suit. This recipe for focaccia, a crisp-on-top, airy bread, is so forgiving that it makes me believe I can bake anything!

Instead of olive oil and balsamic, I love dipping my focaccia into chili crisp. I tried putting chili crisp on top of the focaccia dough before baking, and the result was rather disappointing: The chili flakes got burnt, leaving an unpleasant taste. Instead, I developed a chili crisp–infused oil to use throughout the process. You know that moment of pride you feel after solving a complex math problem? That's exactly how I felt when I came up with this solution. You can even use this oil to dip the focaccia!

On top of the infused oil, the addition of tapioca flour makes this focaccia extra crunchy. Tapioca flour is often used to create a chewy texture. It's the main ingredient in making chewy boba balls. But in this recipe, the flour doesn't turn the bread chewy; instead, it creates a wonderfully crunchy, crisp exterior. If you don't have tapioca flour, you can substitute all-purpose flour, but seeking out tapioca flour is worth it to experience the crunchy ASMR that you don't experience with other focaccia.

MAKES ONE 9 X 13 IN
[23 X 33 CM] LOAF

CHILI CRISP OIL

*1 cup [240 ml]
extra-virgin olive oil*

*¼ cup [60 g] chili crisp,
plus more for serving*

2 Tbsp soy sauce

DOUGH

*One 2¼ tsp [7 g] packet
active dry yeast*

2 Tbsp granulated sugar

*2½ cups [600 ml] warm
water*

*5 cups [700 g] all-purpose
flour*

½ cup [75 g] tapioca flour

1 tsp baking powder

1 Tbsp kosher salt

1 lemon, zested and juiced

1. **To make the chili crisp oil:** In a small pan, add the olive oil, chili crisp, and soy sauce. Simmer it over low heat while stirring for 6 to 8 minutes, or until the oil turns deep red. Pour the mixture through a fine-mesh sieve into a bowl and reserve the solids in the strainer. Set aside the chili crisp–infused oil.

2. **To make the dough:** In a large measuring cup or medium bowl, add the yeast, sugar, and warm water. Whisk to combine and set it aside for 15 minutes, or until bubbles form.

3. In a large bowl, add the all-purpose flour, tapioca flour, baking powder, and salt. Whisk to combine. Pour the warm yeast mixture into the dry ingredients. Using a wooden spoon or a silicone spatula, stir to combine until a rough dough forms.

4. Add about ⅓ cup [80 ml] of the infused oil to a separate large clean bowl and add the dough. Coat the dough in the oil and cover it with a damp kitchen towel. Let rise at room temperature for 4 hours or up to 1 day in the fridge. The dough should be doubled in size.

cont'd.

5. While keeping the dough in the bowl, use two forks to pull the dough from the edge and bring it to the center. Do this for all four sides of the dough while making a quarter turn after each fold, and repeat the same process twice, for three rounds total.

6. Grease a 9 by 13 in [23 by 33 cm] baking pan with ¼ cup [60 ml] of the remaining chili crisp–infused oil. This will yield thicker focaccia, ideal for making sandwiches. Alternatively, you can grease a half-size baking sheet instead, which will create thin focaccia, perfect for breadsticks.

7. Transfer the deflated dough to the prepared baking pan of your choice, and let it rise again, until it's doubled in size, at least 1 hour or up to 3 to 4 hours.

8. Preheat the oven to 425°F [220°C].

9. The dough is ready when it springs back slowly when you poke it. Lightly oil your hands with chili crisp–infused oil. If using a half-size baking sheet, you most likely will have to stretch the dough to fill the surface. With your greased hands, dimple the dough all over with your fingers, creating deep indents throughout the dough.

10. Drizzle about ¼ cup [60 ml] of the remaining chili crisp–infused oil all over the dough. The oil on top will create a nice golden-brown crust. Bake the focaccia for 20 to 25 minutes if using a baking sheet and for 30 to 35 minutes if using a baking pan, or until the top gets golden brown.

11. Meanwhile, in a small bowl, combine the zest and freshly squeezed juice from the lemon and the reserved solids from the chili crisp. Whisk to combine until it's a spreadable liquid mixture.

12. Once the focaccia comes out of the oven, use a spoon to spread the lemony chili crisp mixture all over the bread while it's still hot. Let cool for 5 minutes and slice into squares or rectangles to enjoy. Serve with an extra drizzle of chili crisp if desired. The leftovers can be stored in an airtight container in the freezer for up to 1 month. Reheat them on a baking sheet at 350°F [180°C] for 10 minutes.

NOTE: Extra chili crisp–infused oil is fantastic as a dipping oil for the focaccia. Or use it for frying eggs, finishing pasta, and more.

Cheesy Cornbread
with Green Chiles

Crumbly, honey-soaked cornbread is one of my favorite side dishes, especially when I have a barbecue platter. It's a delicious vehicle to soak up anything saucy or to enjoy alongside well-smoked barbecue meat. I never thought of having cornbread as a stand-alone snack until I made this cheesy cornbread.

The combination of green chiles, chili crisp, and Cheddar cheese creates this highly satisfying blend of flavors and textures that transforms cornbread from a supporting actor to the star who steals the spotlight. A block of Cheddar cheese gets used in two different ways: Cheddar cubes create pockets of melty, cheesy goodness throughout the cornbread, and shredded Cheddar gets sprinkled on top to make a nice, salty, cheesy crust. Chili crisp is subtle but present, while complementing the flavors of the green chiles beautifully.

I enjoy this cheesy cornbread as a pick-me-up afternoon treat, breakfast, or midnight snack. You don't need anything else to enjoy this purely blissful bite, except maybe more chili crisp on top.

MAKES 9 TO 16 SQUARES

1 cup [140 g] cornmeal

1 cup [140 g] all-purpose flour

¼ cup [50 g] granulated sugar

1 Tbsp baking powder

1 tsp kosher salt

1 cup [240 ml] milk

3 Tbsp neutral oil, such as vegetable or canola

2 to 3 Tbsp chili crisp, depending on desired spice level, plus more for serving

1 Tbsp light soy sauce

One 3 ½ oz [100 g] block Cheddar cheese

One 4 oz [115 g] can diced green chiles, drained

¼ cup [55 g] salted butter, plus more for serving

1. Preheat the oven to 425°F [220°C].

2. In a large bowl, add the cornmeal, flour, sugar, baking powder, and salt. Mix to combine.

3. In a separate bowl, add the milk, oil, chili crisp, and soy sauce. Whisk to combine.

4. Combine the wet and dry ingredients, and stir until the batter comes together.

5. Cut the Cheddar cheese block in half. Cut half of the cheese block into small cubes.

Grate the other half on the large holes of a box grater and set aside. Add the cheese cubes and green chiles to the batter and stir to combine.

6. Melt the butter in a microwave. Pour the melted butter into a 9 in [23 cm] square baking pan and swirl it around until the butter coats all the sides. Transfer the batter to the greased baking pan. Using a silicone spatula, spread the batter evenly. Sprinkle the grated Cheddar cheese on top. Bake it for 20 to 25 minutes, or until golden brown.

7. Let cool for 10 minutes, then cut it into nine or sixteen squares. Serve while it's still warm. Pair it with an extra drizzle of chili crisp or a nub of butter. The leftovers can be wrapped and stored at room temperature for up to 3 days or in the freezer for up to 3 months.

Spicy Garlicky Corn Cheese Ciabatta Bread

Garlic bread meets Korean corn cheese! Two of my favorite dishes come together for this intensely garlicky cheese bread. There are three different components to build strong, bold garlic flavors: roasted garlic paste, minced raw garlic, and garlic powder. Roasted garlic paste has a subtle sweetness, while the minced raw garlic has a more pungent, pronounced garlic taste. Then, garlic powder glues all the other garlic flavors together. If you laugh at a recipe that only uses one clove of garlic, this is the one that uses all your garlic!

Then, there's a second portion of the recipe, Korean corn cheese. It's a fairly simple dish that consists of sweet canned corn kernels, lots of mayonnaise, and mozzarella cheese. All these essential ingredients are mixed into the super garlicky paste in this gloriously delicious marriage of two dishes. Chili crisp brings everything together as a cultural bridge that connects a classic Korean side dish and an Italian American staple.

The garlicky corn cheese paste is super jammy, and you can really slather it on anything, such as naan or pizza dough. Be sure to use hearty bread like ciabatta to handle the thick layer of jammy paste. Serve this with Fiery Spaghetti and Meatballs (page 70) for an ultimate feast!

SERVES 4 TO 6

3 whole garlic bulbs, plus 12 garlic cloves, minced (about ¼ cup [35 g])

1½ to 3 Tbsp olive oil

One 15 oz [425 g] can whole kernel corn, drained

½ cup [113 g] unsalted butter, at room temperature

½ cup [50 g] grated Parmesan cheese

¼ cup [60g] chili crisp

3 green onions, chopped

3 Tbsp mayonnaise

1 Tbsp granulated sugar

1½ tsp garlic powder

1½ tsp freshly ground black pepper

12 in [30.5 cm] ciabatta loaf, cut lengthwise

1 cup [120 g] shredded mozzarella

Drizzle of honey (optional)

1. Preheat the oven to 400°F [200°C].

2. Peel the outer layers of the whole garlic bulbs while leaving the bulbs intact. Cut about ½ in [13 mm] from the top of the bulbs to expose the cloves. Cover each bulb with ½ to 1 Tbsp of olive oil. Tightly wrap the garlic with aluminum foil and bake them for 30 to 40 minutes, or until the cloves are browned and feel soft to the touch.

3. Remove the roasted garlic from the oven and increase the oven temperature to 450°F [230°C].

4. Squeeze the softened roasted garlic into a medium bowl and mash it to make a paste. There should be about 2 Tbsp of roasted garlic paste. Add the corn, butter, Parmesan, chili crisp, minced garlic, green onions, mayonnaise, sugar, garlic powder, and pepper. Stir until it combines into a spreadable paste.

cont'd.

5. Halve the ciabatta lengthwise, then cut it in half crosswise to have four pieces total. Slather the garlicky spread on top of the bread, using about ½ cup [roughly around 80 g] per piece. Transfer the bread to a baking sheet and sprinkle with the mozzarella cheese.

6. Bake for 10 to 13 minutes, or until the cheese is melted and the bread is toasted. Serve immediately. If you want to add a little bit of sweetness to balance the garlicky, spicy flavors, add a drizzle of honey (or hot honey!) at the end. The leftovers can be wrapped in aluminum foil and kept in the freezer until ready to eat again. Reheat them in a 400°F [200°C] oven for 10 to 15 minutes.

chapter 3

MEAT, SEAFOOD, AND MORE

CHILI CRISP LOST IN TRANSLATION

"What are you writing a book about?" my Korean parents asked. I hesitantly responded, "Chili oil." Even though I knew chili oil wasn't the same as chili crisp, I struggled to explain more about it. There's no concept of chili crisp in Korean cuisine. They couldn't quite understand what I was writing a book about, while cheering for me. I was happy that I shared this news with them, but something about this moment made me slightly sad.

Talking about food with my parents has been my way of wanting to connect with them. Even though my Korean parents never really taught me how to cook, I would ask them how to make certain dishes as a conversation starter. If I asked them how to make Korean dishes, kimchi jjigae, for example, I would see my mom's eyes light up as she explained her simple recipes, followed by my dad sharing memories of a restaurant that sold a delicious kimchi jjigae. I always treasure those moments of joyful connections around food.

As I was developing chili crisp recipes, I wanted to share the joy of cooking and tasting the spicy condiment with them. Because they had never tasted chili crisp before, they struggled to find things to say to connect with me. I explained the taste of chili crisp and how I would use it in many recipes, but my parents' faces never lit up. My joy of cooking and eating chili crisp was completely lost in translation with my Korean parents.

I tried to find ways to connect with them over my joy of chili crisp. It certainly didn't come easy, unlike meeting other chili crisp fans. I would share videos of me trying some fun recipes, such as my Spicy Tahini Cream Cheese Swirled Brownies (page 149) or Silken Tofu Soup (page 123), one of my parents' favorite soups. I wanted to include some Korean-inspired recipes to make it easier for them to understand. I shared all the fun and not-so-exciting moments of developing recipes with chili crisp with them. When I felt stuck with my process, I wished I could get advice from my parents. I hoped they could be my source of references and inspiration. I couldn't ask my mom her favorite ways of cooking chili crisp. I felt lost and a little lonely when I didn't have many people to talk to about my feelings about it, especially my family.

Despite the language barrier and the lost Korean translation of chili crisp, we kept trying to create moments of connection together. Even though they had never tasted my chili crisp (or any kind, as a matter of fact), they would share flavor suggestions and make comments on presentations. They continued asking me for updates, making me feel as if we were working on this book together indirectly.

I can't wait for us to share joyful, happy chili crisp moments together. Maybe my parents can be the first chili crisp fans in my small hometown in Korea?

Chili Crisp Bulgogi Deopbap

Deopbap is a catchall Korean term that refers to a bowl of rice with some sort of topping. In Korean, *deop* means "covered" and *bap* means "rice." I love this casual rice bowl concept for the toppings, ranging from raw fish (hoe-deopbap) to spicy pork. My topping choice always ends up being bulgogi. Bulgogi ("fiery meat") is one of the most popular Korean dishes. It's typically cooked after being marinated in some sort of sauce that includes soy sauce or gochujang. I put a spin on this Korean comfort dish by introducing chili crisp to the marinade. It adds a pleasant warmth to the dish while harmonizing with other flavors in the marinade. It's slightly different compared to the spicy version of bulgogi made with gochujang thanks to the complex flavors of chili crisp. The oil from the chili crisp makes the sauce taste incredible, especially after it mixes with the flavors from the beef. This will easily be one of your go-to rice bowl dishes, and an extra drizzle of chili crisp at the end is always encouraged.

SERVES 2 TO 4

1 lb [455 g] thinly sliced beef or shaved beef steak (see Note)

2 tsp granulated sugar

2 tsp freshly ground black pepper

3 Tbsp soy sauce

3 Tbsp chili crisp

2 Tbsp honey

1 Tbsp fish sauce

1 Tbsp toasted sesame oil

1 Tbsp rice wine vinegar

4 or 5 garlic cloves, minced

1 medium onion, sliced

4 green onions

Neutral oil, such as vegetable or canola, for frying

Chili Crisp Fried Eggs (page 31), for serving

Cooked rice, for serving

Toasted sesame seeds, for garnish

1. In a medium bowl, season the sliced beef with the sugar and pepper and with clean hands massage the seasonings into the meat thoroughly. This process will ensure that the meat absorbs the marinade better. Add the soy sauce, chili crisp, honey, fish sauce, sesame oil, and rice wine vinegar to the bowl with the meat, along with the garlic and onion. Mix everything together and let the meat marinate for at least 1 hour and up to overnight in the fridge.

2. Cut each of the green onions into four chunks. Cut the thick white parts lengthwise into two pieces. Chop one of the green chunks and reserve for garnish.

3. When you're ready to cook the meat, add a splash of oil to a medium skillet or sauté pan over medium-high heat. Add the sliced green onion chunks to the pan and cook for 1 minute, or until fragrant. Add the marinated meat and ¼ cup [60 ml] of water to make the bulgogi extra saucy, which is ideal for the rice to soak up. Cook for 12 to 15 minutes, or until the meat is fully cooked and the sauce is slightly reduced.

4. While the meat is cooking, make the chili crisp fried eggs. Set them aside.

cont'd.

5. In a serving bowl, add hot rice first. Add generous scoops of bulgogi over the rice, then place the chili crisp fried eggs in the center. Garnish with the reserved chopped green onion and the toasted sesame seeds. Serve warm. The leftovers can be stored in the refrigerator in an airtight container for up to 5 days. The uncooked, marinated meat can last in the refrigerator for 3 days. Or you can freeze the marinated, uncooked bulgogi for up to 2 months.

NOTE: Chili Crisp Bulgogi makes a fantastic centerpiece for an easy Korean barbecue at home. Prepare a perfect lettuce ssam with chili crisp bulgogi, a dollop of ssamjang (a Korean savory condiment), and a few pieces of thinly sliced garlic. Also, you can use the same marinade on different cuts of meat, such as pork and chicken.

You can use other thinly sliced meat for this recipe, such as thinly sliced pork butt. Use presliced meat, compared to slicing it thinly on your own. Some packages may specifically call it bulgogi. If not, make sure that the beef is thinly sliced lengthwise, not as chunks or slabs. You can easily find thinly sliced meat at Asian markets, such as H Mart.

One-Pan Steak *with* Spicy Cream Sauce

An exceptional steak doesn't need anything, but a good sauce can transform an average steak into something phenomenal. Inspired by the peppery, creamy flavors of steak au poivre, this recipe will turn your weeknight steak into something memorable. The luscious sauce has a nice balance of acidity and spice from the white wine and chili crisp. And the heavy cream brings all the elements together to create a savory sauce that's good on any grilled meat. This fiery orange sauce would also be excellent with grilled chicken thighs or even thick pork chops. Because the sauce is made in the same pan that cooks the meat, all the flavor bits stuck on the bottom of the pan make the sauce even more robust. I highly recommend pairing this with a bright, zesty salad to cut down the richness, or mashed potatoes, rice, or even bread to soak up the sauce.

SERVES 2 TO 4

2 lb [910 g] boneless rib eye steaks

Kosher salt

Freshly ground black pepper

1 Tbsp neutral oil, such as vegetable or canola, plus more as needed

3 Tbsp chili crisp

1 Tbsp Dijon mustard

1 Tbsp rice wine vinegar

1 medium yellow onion, finely diced

3 garlic cloves, minced (about 1 Tbsp)

¼ cup [60 ml] heavy cream

1 Tbsp fresh thyme leaves, chopped

¼ cup [60 ml] white wine, preferably Pinot Grigio or Sauvignon Blanc

1. Season the steaks on all sides with lots of salt and pepper. You should use more salt and pepper than you imagine you need. Let the seasoned steaks sit at room temperature for at least 30 minutes and up to 1 hour. Pat both sides of the steaks dry with paper towels.

2. Heat a large skillet or sauté pan, preferably cast iron, over high heat for 2 minutes. Once the pan is smoking hot, add the oil and swirl to coat the surface. Gently lay the steaks in the pan and let them cook without touching for about 4 minutes. You should be able to see the deep brown crust forming on the bottom.

3. Flip the steaks and continue to cook for about 3 minutes. Make sure to render the fat cap on top of the steak if necessary. For medium-rare, the thick part of the meat should register between 125°F [52°C] and 130°F [55°C]. Once the steak is cooked to your desired doneness, remove it from the pan and transfer it to a cutting board to rest while making the pan sauce. Turn off the heat to let the pan cool slightly.

4. In a small bowl, mix together the chili crisp, mustard, and rice wine vinegar.

cont'd.

5. There should be residual fat in the pan from cooking the steaks, but if not, add a splash of oil. Put the pan over medium-low heat. Add the onion and garlic and sauté for 1 minute. Once the diced onion is slightly translucent and the garlic is fragrant, add the chili crisp–mustard sauce to the pan, followed by the heavy cream and chopped fresh thyme. Simmer the mixture for 3 to 5 minutes, or until slightly thickened. Add the white wine to the sauce and cook for 3 to 5 minutes, or until the sauce thickens. Stir to combine. Taste the sauce, and season it with salt and pepper, if necessary. The sauce should be runny but not watery.

6. Cut the well-rested steak against the grain into 1 in [2.5 cm] thick slices, and place them on a serving platter. Pour the pan sauce over the steak. Serve immediately.

Skillet-Roasted Chili Crisp Chicken _and_ Vegetables

SERVES 4 TO 6

⅓ cup [80 ml] extra-virgin olive oil

2 lemons

¼ cup [60 g] chili crisp

2½ Tbsp kosher salt

1 tsp smoked paprika

One 3 lb [1.4 kg] whole young chicken

1½ lb [680 g] peewee potatoes, halved

2 or 3 onions, roughly chopped

1 or 2 carrots, roughly chopped

5¼ oz [150 g] cabbage, roughly chopped

3 green onions

If there's one dish that I can eat every day without getting sick of it, it would be roast chicken. And ever since I learned how to spatchcock chicken—which cuts the cooking time in half and creates an impressive visual of a flattened chicken—I never looked back. There are countless roast chicken recipes out there, but what makes this recipe particularly exciting is the use of a spicy olive oil mixture that checks all the boxes. It has a perfect blend of salt, fat, acid, and heat. The olive oil provides a wonderfully fruity, fatty foundation. A bright lemon, which uses zest and juice, brings the acid, while chili crisp and smoked paprika add a much-needed spicy kick. Then there comes kosher salt to bring everything together. After getting a spicy massage with this nearly perfect spicy oil, the chicken is nestled on a bed of vegetables, which absorbs all the delicious flavors from the chicken. The copious amount of fat, from olive oil and chili crisp, makes the chicken skin extra crispy and creates an addictive sauce. Any hearty root vegetables, like radishes and sweet potatoes, will be fantastic. A bite of spicy, tangy, crispy, insanely juicy roast chicken tastes like chili crisp heaven, and I would be more than happy (in fact, excited!) to eat this chicken every day.

1. Preheat the oven to 450°F [230°C]. Position a rack in the middle of the oven.

2. In a small bowl, combine the olive oil, zest of 1 lemon (about 1 tsp), freshly squeezed juice of 1 lemon (about ¼ cup [60 ml]), chili crisp, 1 Tbsp of the salt, and paprika. Mix everything well and set aside.

3. Pat the chicken dry with a paper towel. Turn it breast-side down, then take out the backbone by cutting through both sides of the spine with a pair of kitchen scissors. (You can save the backbone for making chicken stock later.) Flip the chicken over. Firmly push down on the center part of the chicken breast until you hear the joint bone crack and the chicken lies flat. Season both sides of the chicken generously with about 1 Tbsp of the salt, making sure all surfaces are covered. Let sit for at least 15 minutes. This step will draw the moisture from the chicken, ensuring crispy chicken skin.

cont'd.

4. Meanwhile, add the potatoes, onions, carrots, and cabbage to a 12 in [30 cm] cast-iron sauté pan or skillet. Halve the remaining lemon and slice it about ¼ in [6 mm] thick. Scatter the sliced lemons in the pan with the vegetables. Season the lemon and vegetable mixture with 2 Tbsp of the reserved spicy olive oil mixture and the remaining ½ Tbsp of salt. Toss everything thoroughly, preferably with your clean hands, making sure everything is fully coated with the spicy olive oil.

5. After 15 minutes, there should be some moisture on the salted spatchcocked chicken. Pat both sides dry with a paper towel and arrange it, skin-side down, on top of the vegetables and lemon in the pan.

6. Pour half of the remaining oil inside the chicken, where the bones are, first. Flip the chicken over and pour the remaining oil on the skin side. Use your clean hands to make sure the spicy oil mixture coats the entire surface of the chicken.

7. Bake the chicken in the oven for 40 to 45 minutes, or until the internal temperature reaches 165°F [74°C]. Remove the pan from the oven, cover with aluminum foil, and let it rest for 10 minutes.

8. While the chicken rests, prepare the green onion garnish. Cut each green onion crosswise into thirds, and slice each piece lengthwise into long, thin strips. Place the sliced green onions in a bowl of cold water to keep them crisp.

9. When ready to serve, cut the chicken into quarters or eighths, scatter the sliced green onions around the pan, and place the chicken pieces on top. Serve immediately, directly from the pan. The leftovers can be stored in an airtight container in the fridge for up to 3 days.

NOTE: If you use a sheet pan or a baking pan to make this recipe, instead of a cast-iron pan, be sure to have all the vegetables tucked under the chicken, not on the side, to prevent them from burning.

Spicy, Braised Chicken Legs

Growing up in Korea, I never learned how to cook from my mom, who was very busy with her career. Even though I loved the rare times that my mom cooked, I didn't have many fond memories of watching her cook in the kitchen. So, many nights, my friends' moms invited me over to join their family for dinner. One day, a friend's mom made dak-bokkeum-tang, spicy red braised chicken with vegetables. The juicy chicken, fork-tender potatoes, and carrots arrived at the table in the pot, still bubbling in a spicy broth. It was such a satisfying, hearty, and memorable meal that left a strong impression that I still hold dearly. This addictively spicy and savory chicken dish gave me a taste of different home-cooked meals that I had not experienced with my mom before. Looking back on that memory, I wanted to create something similar to those hearty, comforting flavors of dak-bokkeum-tang, but with my own twists. Chili crisp adds more complex notes of heat in addition to gochujang. Tomato paste adds a slight sweetness, while doenjang adds a subtle funk to the broth. The real trick of this recipe is adding grated potatoes to the broth toward the end, which thickens the broth as it coats the chicken and vegetables. Just like that dinner where I devoured my friend's mom's dak-bokkeum-tang, I eat my feelings with spicy, braised chicken legs every single time I make them.

SERVES 2 OR 3

2 lb [910 g] chicken legs

2 Tbsp granulated sugar

1½ tsp kosher salt

1 tsp freshly ground black pepper

3 or 4 medium potatoes, peeled

1 medium yellow onion, peeled

1 medium carrot, peeled

5 green onions

1 Tbsp neutral oil, such as vegetable or canola

½ cup [120 ml] soy sauce

¼ cup [60 g] chili crisp

2 Tbsp mirin

1½ tsp gochujang

1½ tsp tomato paste

1½ tsp doenjang

5 or 6 garlic cloves, minced

Cooked rice, for serving

1. In a medium bowl, add the chicken legs, season them with the sugar, salt, and pepper, and mix well so that each chicken leg is coated with the seasonings. Let them sit for at least 15 minutes while preparing the vegetables and marinade. This process helps the chicken absorb the marinade better.

2. Set aside one peeled potato, preferably a small or medium one, then cut the potatoes, onion, and carrot into rough bite-size pieces (bigger chunks will keep their shape as they braise in the sauce). Slice four of the green onions into 3 in [7.5 cm] pieces.

3. In a large heavy-bottom pot over medium-low heat, add the oil and seasoned chicken legs. Stir the chicken for 3 to 5 minutes, or until light brown, then add the soy sauce, chili crisp, and mirin, scraping up any brown bits from the pan with a spatula.

4. Add 1 cup [240 ml] of water to the pot, followed by the carrots, onions, potatoes, and green onion pieces. Turn the heat to high and add the gochujang, tomato paste, and doenjang, mixing until dissolved in the water. Simmer the chicken and the vegetables for 15 to 20 minutes, while occasionally stirring to prevent any burning.

5. While the chicken and the vegetables simmer, grate the reserved peeled potato. After 20 minutes of simmering, or when the chicken legs look tender and almost cooked, add the grated potatoes and minced garlic to the broth and mix well. Continue to simmer for 5 to 7 minutes, or until the broth gets slightly thick.

6. Chop the remaining green onion and sprinkle it over the chicken. Serve immediately with a side of rice. The leftovers can be stored in an airtight container in the fridge for up to 3 days. Reheat them in a microwave, or add a little water or stock and reheat them on the stove.

Spicy Pork Belly Stir-Fry *with* Celery

I still remember my first time trying grilled pork belly with chili crisp. The tangy, spicy flavors from chili crisp created a delicious harmony with the fatty, slightly charred pork belly. It was a phenomenal flavor combo that I couldn't forget. Since then, I have always served chili crisp as one of the dipping sauces at my Korean barbecue parties. Spicy pork isn't anything new to many cuisines, especially Korean. In fact, one of my favorite Korean dishes is duru chigi, a spicy Korean pork belly dish that's stir-fried with lots of seasonings. Instead of using gochujang and gochugaru, essential ingredients to make duru chigi, I leaned into the flavors of chili crisp to bring the heat and savory notes. Other umami-forward seasonings like soy sauce and oyster sauce add another depth of flavor to the sauce. But what makes this dish unique is celery. When sliced celery is cooked in chili crisp–infused pork fat, it helps cut through the fattiness and adds a deliciously bitter crunch, balancing the overall textures. I love serving this over a bowl of rice or noodles. Or even better, serve this as an easy, at-home Korean barbecue centerpiece with lettuce and dipping sauces.

1. In a small bowl, mix the chili crisp, soy sauce, mirin, oyster sauce, and rice wine vinegar to make the seasoning sauce. Set aside.

2. In a large skillet or sauté pan over medium-high heat, add the oil and pork belly. Season it with the salt, ginger, and sugar and cook for 3 to 5 minutes, or until the pork belly is no longer pink and has a light brown crust. Add the green onions and garlic and cook for 1 minute, or until they become fragrant.

3. Pour the sauce into the pan and stir-fry everything for 5 to 7 minutes, or until the pork belly absorbs all the sauce.

4. Add the celery to the skillet with the pork and stir-fry for 3 to 5 minutes, or until the celery starts to look slightly translucent. Garnish with toasted sesame seeds.

5. Serve immediately with a side of rice or cooked noodles. The leftovers can be stored in an airtight container in the fridge for up to 4 days.

SERVES 3 OR 4

¼ cup [60 g] chili crisp

2 Tbsp soy sauce

2 Tbsp mirin

1 Tbsp oyster sauce

1 Tbsp rice wine vinegar

1 tsp neutral oil, such as vegetable or canola

1 lb [455 g] sliced pork belly, cut into bite-size pieces (see Note)

1 tsp kosher salt

1 tsp ground ginger

1 Tbsp granulated sugar

¾ cup [36 g] chopped green onions (about 4)

5 garlic cloves, minced

1 head celery, halved and sliced into 2 in [5 cm] long pieces

Toasted sesame seeds, for garnish

Warm rice or cooked noodles, for serving

NOTE: When buying pork belly, be sure to get the sliced skinless one that's prepared for Korean barbecue rather than a thick slab of pork belly (which will cook unevenly). The ideal thickness for this recipe is ¼ in [6 mm].

Panko-Crusted Baked Salmon

I have to admit: Salmon was not in my regular meal rotation for a long time. I always went for meatier protein options like chicken and pork. But since I've made this recipe, that narrative has completely changed. It has so much flavor and exciting texture in each bite, and it could easily win against any other meaty dishes I cook. My favorite component of this recipe is the salty-spicy-bright seasoning paste. It also adheres the crispy panko crust, made with green onions, minced garlic, and a drizzle of toasted sesame oil, to the salmon. So, as the crust gets baked, its aromatics infuse into the fish. You get the crispy crunch from panko first, then umami-rich, slightly tangy, flaky salmon follows. It's an easy yet impressive weeknight meal that has me adding salmon to my grocery list every single week. Every time I eat this, I have a big smile on my face, and I know you will feel the same too.

SERVES 2

2 Tbsp Kewpie mayo

1½ Tbsp chili crisp

1½ tsp oyster sauce

1 lemon, zested and juiced

½ cup [40 g] panko

¼ cup [12 g] chopped green onions (about 2)

2 garlic cloves, minced

1 Tbsp toasted sesame oil

1 lb [455 g] boneless salmon fillet, halved

1 tsp kosher salt

¼ tsp freshly ground black pepper

2 Tbsp neutral oil, such as vegetable or canola

1. Preheat the oven to 400°F [200°C].

2. In a small bowl, combine the mayo, chili crisp, oyster sauce, and lemon zest. Whisk everything together until smooth.

3. In a separate bowl, combine the panko, the white parts of the green onions, garlic, and sesame oil and mix until well combined.

4. Pat the salmon dry with paper towels and set skin-side down on the cutting board. Season both sides with the salt and pepper. Then, using a brush or a spoon, smother the mayo–chili crisp sauce on top of the salmon.

5. Sprinkle the seasoned panko on top of the smothered salmon. Using your clean hands or a measuring spoon, press down the panko mixture so that it sticks to the salmon.

6. In a 12 in [30 cm] cast-iron skillet or large, ovenproof skillet over medium-high heat, heat the neutral oil. When the oil gets hot, place the prepared salmon in the pan, skin-side down, and sear for 3 to 4 minutes, or until you see the edges of the skin on the bottom start to brown.

7. Transfer the skillet to the preheated oven and bake the salmon for 5 to 7 minutes, or until it's firm to the touch and flakes with a fork. The thickest part of the fish should register between 125°F [51°C] and 130°F [54°C] on a meat thermometer for medium-cooked salmon. If you want to cook the salmon slightly more, the internal temperature can go up to 140°F [60°C], but be sure not to go above that temperature to avoid overcooked fish.

8. Serve the baked salmon right away, and garnish with the green parts from the green onions. Squeeze lemon on top of the salmon right before serving for the extra zing of brightness.

Panzanella *with a* Twist

The best part of eating panzanella is getting a bite of crispy bread cubes that soak up the tangy vinaigrette with juicy tomatoes. Here, I take it up a notch by mixing chili crisp into the golden-brown bread cubes to add the right amount of heat and savory notes to this refreshing salad. You might think adding chili crisp would make the salad spicy. But cucumbers, tomatoes, and bell peppers are hefty and can handle the seasonings without losing their fresh crunch and the warmth of the chili crisp delightfully enhances and complements them. You can use one type of tomato, but I love mixing different sizes and varieties for more textures and colors. The spice of chili crisp in the tangy vinaigrette makes each bite even more satisfying.

1. **To make the crispy bread cubes:** In a large skillet or sauté pan over medium-low heat, add the olive oil. Working in batches, add the bread cubes to the pan, just enough to cover the bottom. Be sure not to overcrowd. Lightly fry them, frequently tossing, for 5 minutes, or until the sides are nicely browned. Repeat with the remaining bread cubes until all are equally cooked and lightly fried. Transfer the bread cubes to a large bowl and drizzle the chili crisp on them while still hot. Toss thoroughly so that the chili crisp fully coats the crispy bread cubes. Set aside.

2. **To make the vinaigrette:** In a medium bowl, add the rice vinegar, chili crisp, mustard, salt, pepper, lemon zest (roughly 1 tsp), and lemon juice (roughly ¼ cup [60 ml]) and whisk everything to combine. While whisking, drizzle in the olive oil to emulsify the sauce.

3. **To make the salad:** In a large bowl, mix both tomatoes, cucumber, bell pepper, red onion, and basil. Add the bread cubes and pour in about half of the vinaigrette. Toss thoroughly. Taste and season with more vinaigrette, salt, and pepper if desired.

4. Let sit for 20 to 30 minutes before serving to soak up the dressing.

5. The leftovers can be stored in an airtight container at room temperature for up to 1 day. You can refrigerate it, but it will affect the texture of the tomatoes and bread cubes.

NOTE: I recommend sourdough, but you can use any bread, as long as it can get browned and crispy, like croutons.

SERVES 8 TO 10

CRISPY BREAD CUBES

3 Tbsp extra-virgin olive oil

3 cups [275 g] cubed sourdough (1 in [2.5 cm] cubes) (see Note)

2 Tbsp chili crisp

VINAIGRETTE

3 Tbsp rice vinegar

3 Tbsp chili crisp

1 tsp Dijon mustard

½ tsp kosher salt

¼ tsp freshly ground black pepper

1 lemon, zested and juiced

½ cup [120 ml] extra-virgin olive oil

SALAD

2 large tomatoes, cut into 1 in [2.5 cm] cubes

1 pint [455 g] heirloom cherry tomatoes

1 English cucumber, unpeeled, seeded, and cut into ½ in [13 mm] slices

1 cup [120 g] chopped bell pepper (1 in [2.5 cm] pieces)

½ red onion, thinly sliced

30 fresh basil leaves, julienned

Spicy Seafood Stir-Fry *over* Rice

I always keep handy mixed bags of seafood such as calamari, mussels, shrimp, and even scallops in my freezer. I love adding a handful of a frozen seafood blend to fried rice and soups without even thawing. And this recipe showcases the magic of this freezer staple. It gets tossed with this addictively spicy, peppery sauce and crunchy vegetables like cabbage and carrots. The key to making a delicious seafood stir-fry, especially when using a frozen seafood blend, is to cook out all the extra moisture. The fiery flavors of the dish are inspired by one of my favorite spicy noodle dishes, jjamppong, but without broth. The different textures from the frozen seafood blend make each bite extra exciting. The drizzle of toasted sesame oil at the end makes a big difference, so don't skip it! Whether you serve this over rice or noodles, this dish will whet your appetite.

1. Rinse the frozen seafood blend in a colander under running water to help it defrost. Let it drain in the colander while you prepare the vegetables.

2. In a medium bowl, combine the chili crisp, garlic, soy sauce, mirin, oyster sauce, ginger, and pepper.

3. In a large skillet or sauté pan over medium-high heat, add the neutral oil. Add 3 Tbsp of the green onions to the pan and cook for 1 minute, or until fragrant. Add the drained, partially defrosted seafood blend to the pan. The seafood will expel a lot of moisture. Stir and cook the mixture for 3 to 5 minutes, or until most of the moisture is evaporated. You don't want it to be watery, only slightly moist.

4. Once there's barely any moisture left in the pan, add the chili crisp mixture, sugar, cabbage, carrot, and onion. Sauté everything for 3 to 5 minutes, or until the vegetables are tender but not mushy.

5. Meanwhile, make a slurry by mixing the potato starch and 1 Tbsp of water. Add the slurry to the pan and sauté for a few minutes, or until the mixture is slightly thickened. Turn off the heat and drizzle with the toasted sesame oil. Mix to combine.

6. Serve the mixture over rice and garnish with the remaining 1 Tbsp of chopped green onion, the toasted sesame seeds, and an extra drizzle of chili crisp, if desired. The leftovers can be stored in an airtight container in the fridge for up to 5 days.

SERVES 3 OR 4

1 lb [455 g] frozen seafood blend

¼ cup [60 g] chili crisp, plus more for drizzling

6 garlic cloves, minced (about 2 Tbsp)

3 Tbsp soy sauce

3 Tbsp mirin

1 Tbsp oyster sauce

1 tsp ground ginger

1 tsp freshly ground black pepper

1 Tbsp neutral oil, such as vegetable or canola

4 Tbsp [12 g] chopped green onions (about 2)

1 tsp granulated sugar

¾ cup [45 g] sliced cabbage leaves, cut lengthwise

½ cup [50 g] shredded carrot

1 medium onion, sliced

1 Tbsp potato starch or cornstarch

1 tsp toasted sesame oil

Cooked rice, for serving

Toasted sesame seeds, for garnish

Steamed Mussels *with* Tomato Chili Crisp Broth

Cleaning bivalves can be a hassle, but it's absolutely worth the effort for these spicy, steamed mussels. Tomato paste gets caramelized with butter to bring a slight sweetness. Then, the combination of fire-roasted crushed tomatoes, white wine, and slightly briny juice from the mussels creates a glorious broth that demands to be soaked up with slices of grilled baguette. Be sure to use fresh mussels for this, rather than frozen ones, to get the flavorful juice that comes from steaming mussels. Feel free to use other shellfish, such as clams and even shrimp. The addictive, tomato-heavy chili crisp broth can embrace all types of seafood.

SERVES 4

2 Tbsp unsalted butter

1 medium yellow onion, finely diced

3 garlic cloves, minced (about 1 Tbsp)

2 Tbsp tomato paste

One 28 oz [795 g] can fire-roasted diced tomatoes

1 cup [240 ml] white wine, such as Pinot Grigio, Sauvignon Blanc, or Chardonnay

⅓ cup [70 g] chili crisp

2 lb [910 g] mussels, scrubbed and debearded

Olive oil, for grilling

Sliced baguette, for serving

2 Tbsp chopped green onion (about 1)

Lemon wedges, for serving

1. In a heavy-bottom pot over medium-low heat, melt the butter. Add the onion and garlic and cook for 3 to 5 minutes, or until fragrant. Add the tomato paste and cook for 1 minute, or until slightly caramelized. Add the fire-roasted diced tomatoes, white wine, and chili crisp. Stir to combine. Simmer for 10 to 15 minutes, or until the tomato liquid has slightly reduced to let the flavors develop. Add the clean mussels, cover the pot, and cook until all the shells are open, about 5 minutes.

2. While the mussels are simmering in the broth, grill the bread. In a sauté pan or skillet, preferably cast iron, over medium-high heat, lightly drizzle the pan with olive oil and add the baguette slices. Cook each side for 2 minutes, or until golden brown.

3. Before serving, discard any unopened shells in the pot. Garnish with the chopped green onion and squeeze the lemon wedges over the mussels right before serving. Serve it with the grilled bread.

4. If there are any leftovers, separate the mussel meat from the shells, mix them with the remaining sauce, and store in an airtight container in the refrigerator for up to 2 days.

Oven-Braised Cod *and* Kale in Chili-Chipotle Broth

SERVES 2 TO 4

2 large red onions

2 large tomatoes, cut into quarters

¼ cup [60 g] chili crisp

One 7 oz [200 g] can chipotle peppers in adobo sauce

5 garlic cloves

Kosher salt

1 Tbsp extra-virgin olive oil

Freshly ground black pepper

One 13½ oz [400 ml] can full-fat coconut milk

2 tsp potato starch or cornstarch

1 bunch lacinato kale, roughly chopped

1 tsp fish sauce

1½ lb [680 g] cod fillets, cut into 3 in [7.5 cm] chunks

3 Tbsp roughly chopped fresh cilantro, for garnish

Cooked jasmine rice or grilled bread, for serving

Here's a flavor pairing that I get excited about: chipotle peppers and chili crisp. If your first reaction is "that's genius!" you get me and I love you for that. If you are skeptical about this, hear me out. Both ingredients bring heat to the dish. But chipotle peppers, especially those that come in a can with adobo sauce, add intense smoky flavors while chili crisp adds a punch of umami. When these two ingredients are combined, it becomes this incredibly smoky, flavorful, goes-well-with-everything sauce. Think of it as a distant cousin of salsa roja! This recipe celebrates the vibrant flavors of the chipotle–chili crisp sauce and welcomes creamy coconut milk to become a cooking liquid for flaky cod and hearty kale. Cod fillets absorb the sauce beautifully, and the lacinato kale makes the dish extra satisfying. Any white fish, like tilapia, will go great in the sauce, as would chicken thighs. I highly recommend serving this with any starch, like jasmine rice or grilled bread, for sopping up the sauce, but even alone this is an easy yet impressive dish.

1. Preheat the oven at 450°F [230°C].

2. Cut one of the onions into 2 in [5 cm] chunks. In an ovenproof skillet or on a baking sheet, add the onion chunks and tomatoes and roast them in the oven for 15 minutes, or until they are softened and slightly charred. Lower the oven temperature to 400°F [200°C].

3. Once the onion and tomatoes are charred, add them to a food processor with the chili crisp, canned chipotle peppers in adobo sauce, garlic, and 1 Tbsp of salt. Pulse for a few seconds so that it's blended but still chunky. Set it aside.

4. Slice the remaining onion. Reserve about a quarter of the sliced onion for garnish. In the ovenproof skillet or a sauté pan, heat the olive oil over medium heat. Add the sliced onion to the pan, season it with 1 tsp of freshly ground black pepper, and cook for 2 minutes, or until fragrant and soft. Add 1 cup [240 g] of the chipotle–chili crisp sauce to the pan. Cook, frequently stirring, until fragrant, 3 to 4 minutes. This process will deepen the flavors of the chipotle–chili crisp sauce.

5. Meanwhile, in a medium bowl, whisk the coconut milk, potato starch, and ½ tsp of salt to combine.

6. Turn the heat down to low and pour the coconut milk mixture into the pan. Add the kale, stir to combine, and bring to a simmer. Add the fish sauce and continue simmering for 3 to 5 minutes, or until the kale is wilted and tender.

7. Pat the cod dry with paper towels and season with salt and pepper. Carefully place the cod fillets in the pan on the bed of kale. Bake in the oven for 15 to 20 minutes, or until the fish easily flakes with a fork.

8. Garnish the fish with the reserved sliced red onion and cilantro. Serve it with cooked jasmine rice or grilled bread to soak up the sauce.

9. The leftovers can be stored in an airtight container in the fridge for up to 3 days. Chipotle–chili crisp sauce leftovers can also be refrigerated in an airtight container for up to 1 week. The sauce is fantastic with tortilla chips, served as a salsa, or mixed with mayonnaise to make a delicious, creamy condiment.

Cheesy Chili Crisp–Braised Pork Ribs

I have many happy food memories from growing up in Korea. I specifically remember this one time when I asked my parents to take me to a new restaurant that served spicy braised ribs covered with mozzarella cheese. The image of ribs coated with bright red, intimidatingly spicy sauce was engraved in my hungry and curious elementary-school-student mind. When my mom finally took me to the restaurant and let me feast, I was happily in pain, sweating over these insanely spicy ribs. As a child who hadn't eaten ribs often back then, I was blown away by how a hunk of meat attached to the bone could taste so tender and how flavorful the sweet-and-spicy sauce could be. So, when I eat spicy braised pork ribs, I always think of that nearly life-changing experience.

The meat in this recipe is incredibly tender while keeping its structure. The sauce gets extra umami and savory flavors from the chili crisp, making it exquisite. The double cleaning process to remove any impurities from the ribs is very important for this recipe, but trust me, it's worth the effort. And the sauce, arguably the best part of the recipe, gets its natural sweetness from the onion and apple mixture and its nuanced spice from the chili crisp and gochujang. The sauce will go great with any starch, like noodles and rice, but long, cylindrical rice cakes are the best vehicle to enjoy its flavors. Be sure to dip the spicy, tender ribs in the pool of melty mozzarella cheese in the middle. I still feel like that overly enthusiastic, joyful child whenever I make this recipe.

SERVES 3 OR 4

2 lb [910 g] pork spareribs (St. Louis-style spareribs), cut into individual ribs if a slab

6 green onions

3 bay leaves

2 tsp ground ginger

10 black peppercorns

⅓ cup [80 ml] mirin

⅓ cup [80 ml] maple syrup

1 medium yellow onion, cut into chunks

1 apple, cut into chunks (any type of sweet red apple, such as Honeycrisp or Fuji)

⅓ cup [70 g] chili crisp

9 garlic cloves, minced (about 3 Tbsp)

3 Tbsp soy sauce

3 Tbsp oyster sauce

3 Tbsp gochujang

1 lb [455 g] long, cylindrical rice cakes (tteok)

1 cup [80 g] shredded mozzarella cheese

Cooked rice or noodles, for serving

1. First, soak the pork ribs in water for about an hour to remove any residual blood. Discard the water and clean the ribs under running water to remove any impurities, especially around the bones.

2. In a heavy-bottom pot, add the ribs and enough water to submerge the ribs completely. Using your hands, break apart three of the green onions with the roots attached and add them to the pot, along with the bay leaves, 1 tsp of the ground ginger, and the peppercorns.

3. Once the water boils, cook the ribs for 10 to 15 minutes, or until no more impurities float to the top while skimming them off. Drain the ribs in a colander and wash the ribs under running water, especially around the end bones where there might be blood. Discard all the aromatics for parboiling the ribs. Clean the pot.

cont'd.

4. In the same pot, add the clean, parboiled ribs and enough water to barely cover the ribs. Turn the heat to medium-high. Add the mirin, the remaining ground ginger, and maple syrup and bring to a boil. Turn the heat to medium-low and simmer for 15 to 20 minutes so that the ribs absorb the sweetness before the spicy seasoning paste is added.

5. While the ribs are simmering, make the seasoning sauce. In a food processor, add the onion and apple chunks and process until they become liquid. Pour the mixture into a medium bowl. Add the chili crisp, garlic, soy sauce, oyster sauce, and gochujang.

6. Pour the seasoning mixture over the ribs and cook, stirring occasionally to prevent sticking, for an hour or more. The sauce will be significantly reduced as the ribs soak up the flavors.

7. After about an hour, the meat should be fork-tender and there should be enough sauce to make it look saucy but not brothy. If there's not enough sauce, add more water. If the sauce seems too brothy, cook it longer until has a sauce-like consistency.

8. Cut two of the remaining green onions into 3 in [7.5 cm] chunks. Finely chop the remaining green onion and set it aside for garnish.

9. Add the rice cakes and green onion chunks to the pot with the simmering sauce and ribs, and place them under the ribs. Cook them for 3 to 5 minutes, or until the rice cakes are soft and chewy.

10. Move the ribs to the sides of the pot to create an empty space in the middle. Turn the heat to low and sprinkle the mozzarella cheese in that space to create a melty cheese pool. Cover the pot and let the steam and heat from the simmering sauce melt the cheese for 2 to 3 minutes.

11. Garnish with the reserved chopped green onions and serve with rice or noodles to soak up the spicy sauce. The leftovers can be stored in an airtight container in the fridge for up to 4 days.

NOTE: If there's too much broth left over, toss noodles (like udon) in them! You've basically created another delicious dish. Or use the leftover broth as a base for making delicious, porky, flavorful ramen at home.

Savory Mushroom *and* Ground Beef Ssam

Ssam, meaning "wrapped" in Korean, refers to a popular style of eating in Korean cuisine. It's typically made with any type of leafy vegetables, like lettuce and perilla leaves (kkaetnip), wrapped around a piece of meat (or many other fillings). What makes a good ssam depends on what goes in it, and this savory mushroom and ground meat combination makes each bite delightfully satisfying. Shiitake mushrooms already have a meaty texture, so they seamlessly blend with ground beef. And they become a great canvas to absorb the salty, tangy sauce with a bit of heat. Tomato paste brings a hint of caramelization as it cooks with the meat.

Here's what I recommend so that you can have your perfect ssam: Mix some of the savory mushroom and ground beef with rice first. Then, flatten a few lettuce leaves in the palms of your hands. Add mixed rice in the center of the greens, followed by a scoop of the remaining savory mushroom and meat mixture. Wrap it up like a delicious pouch, and taste the perfection in one big, joyful bite.

SERVES 2 TO 4

8 oz [230 g] shallots

1 cup [240 ml] neutral oil, such as vegetable or canola

¼ cup [12 g] chopped green onions (about 2)

3 garlic cloves, minced (about 1 Tbsp)

1 lb [455 g] ground beef

8 oz [230 g] fresh shiitake mushrooms, chopped into bite-size pieces

1 medium yellow onion, sliced

¼ cup [60 g] chili crisp

3 Tbsp soy sauce

1 Tbsp tomato paste

1 Tbsp rice wine vinegar

1 tsp granulated sugar

½ cup [20 g] chopped fresh cilantro leaves and stems

Toasted sesame seeds, for garnish

Cooked rice, for serving

Lettuce or any leafy vegetables, for serving

Ssamjang (Korean spicy dipping sauce), for serving

1. Using a mandoline, slice the shallots into thin, uniform rounds.

2. In a medium saucepan over medium-high heat, heat the oil. Look for the bubbles to rise, and add a small piece of sliced shallot as a test. Once it's frying up, add the rest of sliced shallots and lightly fry them, occasionally stirring, for 9 to 11 minutes, or until crispy and golden brown. Place a sieve over a medium bowl and pour the fried shallots into it to drain, reserving the oil. Line a plate with paper towels and transfer the fried shallots to the plate to drain further. Set aside for garnish.

3. In a large skillet or a cast-iron pan over high heat, add 2 Tbsp of the reserved shallot oil and the green onions and cook for 1 minute, or until fragrant. Add the garlic and cook for 1 minute more. When the aromatics are fragrant, add the ground beef and cook for 2 minutes. While cooking, break up the beef with a wooden spoon or a spatula into smaller pieces. Then add the shiitakes and sliced onion. Cook everything for 4 to 6 minutes, or until the onion starts to be translucent and the mushrooms begin to pick up color.

cont'd.

4. Meanwhile, in a small bowl, combine the chili crisp, soy sauce, tomato paste, rice wine vinegar, and sugar. Add to the meat mixture in the pan and continue to cook for 2 to 3 minutes, or until all the seasonings are fully absorbed into the meat. Turn off the heat, sprinkle with the chopped cilantro, and mix everything together.

5. Garnish with the reserved fried shallots and the toasted sesame seeds. Serve with rice, lettuce, and a dollop of ssamjang to enjoy it as a lettuce wrap, or so-called ssam in Korean. The leftovers can be stored in an airtight container in the fridge for up to 3 days.

NOTE: You can use the remaining shallot-frying oil for regular use. Because it's infused with oniony, shallot taste, it will enhance anything you cook in it.

Dubu Jorim (Braised Tofu)

Tofu is such a versatile ingredient to cook. You can deep-fry or sauté it and even eat it raw. One of my favorite tofu dishes is dubu jorim, Korean braised tofu in a gochujang-forward sauce. Inspired by that dish's techniques and flavors, I let the savory qualities of chili crisp shine in this version. Kimchi adds a slight tang, as well as another layer of heat. Be sure to use firm or extra-firm tofu for this dish so that the tofu planks can hold their shape while braising. The final result has all the qualities that I love about dubu jorim; it's spicy, balanced, and so comforting, especially with a side of rice.

1. Cut the tofu into ½ in [13 mm] thick planks. Transfer them to a plate, season them with the salt, and let them sit for 5 minutes. This process will help the tofu absorb the sauce better when braised. Drain the excess moisture from the tofu.

2. Meanwhile, in a small bowl, combine the chili crisp, garlic, kimchi juice, soy sauce, fish sauce, miso, sugar, gochujang, mirin, and toasted sesame oil to make the sauce. Set aside.

3. In a large skillet or sauté pan over medium-high heat, add the neutral oil. Reserve 2 Tbsp of the chopped green onions and, once the oil is hot, add the rest to the pan. Cook for 1 minute, or until fragrant. Then add the sliced onion and kimchi and sauté everything for 2 to 3 minutes, or until the onions are translucent and the kimchi starts to look tender and slightly brown. Spread the ingredients evenly in the pan, then top with the tofu planks. Pour the reserved sauce over the tofu planks, followed by 1 cup [240 ml] of water.

4. Lower the heat to medium and let it simmer for 10 to 15 minutes, or until most of the liquid has evaporated. It should be saucy, not brothy. Garnish with the reserved green onions. Serve warm with a side of rice.

NOTE: You can omit the fish sauce and add more soy sauce if you want to make this dish vegetarian.

SERVES 2 OR 3

1 lb [455 g] firm tofu

1 tsp kosher salt

¼ cup [60 g] chili crisp

4 garlic cloves, minced

2 Tbsp napa cabbage kimchi juice

1 Tbsp soy sauce

1 Tbsp fish sauce (see Note)

1 Tbsp miso

1½ tsp granulated sugar

1½ tsp gochujang

1 tsp mirin

1 tsp toasted sesame oil

1 Tbsp neutral oil, such as vegetable or canola

¾ cup [36 g] chopped green onions (about 4)

½ medium yellow onion, sliced

½ cup [150 g] chopped napa cabbage kimchi

Cooked rice, for serving

Silken Tofu Soup

Silken tofu and chili crisp go perfectly together, so why not make it into a soup? Soondubu jjigae, Korean silken tofu soup, is one of the most comforting soups. How can you not love that jiggly, custardy, pudding-like texture of silken tofu bubbling in spicy bright red broth? I used chili crisp instead of making the regular soondubu jjigae seasoning paste, and the result was a delicious hybrid of soondubu jjigae and mapo tofu (page 61). Chili crisp creates delicious puddles of spicy oil floating on top of the broth. The use of anchovy fillets in oil mimics the anchovy-dashi broth commonly used in Korean cuisine, without any extra effort. This will be your new go-to soup that feels like getting a big, cozy hug.

One 2 oz [55 g] can anchovy fillets in oil (preferably Cento brand), minced and oil reserved for cooking (see Note)

½ cup [24 g] chopped green onions (about 3)

1 medium yellow onion, sliced

6 garlic cloves, minced (about 2 Tbsp)

3 Tbsp chili crisp

2 Tbsp gochugaru

3 cups [720 ml] chicken broth

2 lb [910 g] silken tofu

1 Tbsp fish sauce, plus more if needed

2 tsp toasted sesame oil

2 to 4 large eggs (1 per portion)

Cooked rice, for serving

1. In a medium heavy-bottom pot over medium-low heat, add the oil from the canned anchovy fillets and heat for 1 minute. Once the oil is hot, add the minced anchovy fillets. Reserve 2 Tbsp of the green onions and add the rest of the green onions and the sliced onion to the pan. Cook everything for 3 to 5 minutes, or until the onion starts to look translucent. Add the garlic and cook for about 30 seconds. Add the chili crisp and gochugaru to the pot and stir everything to make sure the oil from the chili crisp is dispersed throughout the pot. Cook for 2 to 3 minutes. Be sure not to burn. Once the spices have bloomed and the smell of chili flakes is fragrant, pour in the chicken broth. Let the broth simmer for 10 to 15 minutes, or until the onion is cooked and the minced anchovy fillets disappear.

2. Cut the silken tofu into big chunks, add them to the pot, and simmer for another 8 to 10 minutes, or until the tofu warms up and absorbs all the flavors from the broth. Add the fish sauce and toasted sesame oil while it simmers. Season the broth with more fish sauce if necessary.

3. When ready to serve, bring the mixture to a hard boil by incrasing the heat. Right before serving, crack a whole egg into each serving bowl. Ladle hot, hard-boiling broth right on top of the raw eggs so that the heat from the boiling soup poaches the egg. Garnish the soup with the reserved green onions. Serve it with a bowl of rice.

> **NOTE:** I encourage you to use canned anchovy fillets that typically come in 2 oz [55 g] tins, rather than the ones that come in a jar, to get the right amount of oil needed for the soup.

chapter 4

SIDE DISHES

A LOVE LETTER TO LAO GAN MA SPICY CHILI CRISP

What's your favorite chili crisp? I get asked this question all the time. Of course, I love my own chili crisp the most. Not to toot my own horn, but Everyday Savory Chili Crisp (page 18) has the perfect flavors and textures that check all the boxes on my chili crisp scorecard. So, the real question becomes, what's your favorite store-bought chili crisp? Then, my answer is always Lao Gan Ma Spicy Chili Crisp.

You know, we never forget about the first time. Our first kiss, our first love, and the list go on. But, out of many vivid, happy memories in my life, first tastes are moments that I can never forget. And, rightfully, the first taste of Lao Gan Ma Spicy Chili Crisp changed my life for good. I still remember picking up the red jar for the first time. I've seen thousands of food labels, but I was fascinated by the face of a Chinese lady, Tao Huabi, who created the Lao Gan Ma empire. She wasn't even smiling! But, I was drawn to the visible chili flakes, chili oil floating on top, and her somewhat serious face, and just like that, I bought my first Lao Gan Ma Spicy Chili Crisp.

When I opened the jar, its unique, insanely savory aroma hit my nose immediately. Then, without any accompaniments, I tried it by the spoonful. I felt as if something was unlocked inside of me for the first time. As a Korean immigrant living in New York, I had never tasted anything like this. As if I were under a spell, I kept eating more and more by the spoonful. I couldn't get enough of each element of spicy chili crisp: textured chili flakes, the dynamic, complex layers of flavors, a gentle heat that wasn't spicy but rather savory, and crunchy soybeans that absorbed all the flavors!

That life-changing moment with Lao Gan Ma was the beginning of my chili crisp journey. I immediately started talking about it with my friends, who were more familiar with this magical condiment, and they told me all of their favorite ways to enjoy it. Talking about Lao Gan Ma helped me break down the emotional walls with the people around me and build a mutual connection. If I see a jar of

Lao Gan Ma in my friend's fridge, I immediately feel like it's my home. Finding jars of Lao Gan Ma Spicy Chili Crisp at grocery stores gives me this comfort that I can't seem to explain. This Chinese condiment has helped me find my own community as a symbol of shared Asian pride.

Even though my chili crisp collection begins to expand every day with new products, I always come back to Lao Gan Ma. It's the familiarity, comfort, and even nostalgia that I associate with happy memories. No matter how many jars I've gone through since that first time, each jar tastes consistently delicious and incredible, just like the first jar I tasted many years ago. I feel that chili crisp joy when I try new brands. But, it can't be compared to the comfort, satisfaction, and happiness that I feel from eating Lao Gan Ma, which tastes like home. Because it was impossible for me to test all the recipes in this book with every type of chili crisp available in stores, I've made every single recipe in the book with Lao Gan Ma Spicy Chili Crisp, and all of them work delightfully with Lao Gan Ma. And, compared to many chili crisps, Lao Gan Ma is not spicy at all, so you really can load up in these recipes.

It's my way of ensuring that the mother of chili crisp, Tao Huabi, approves of my approach. After all, I can never escape from wanting Asian moms to approve of me, whether that's my real Korean mom or my fairy spicy godmother, Tao Huabi.

Thank you, Lao Gan Ma, for opening the door of this thrilling chili crisp journey. Thank you for helping me embrace my Asian identity. Thank you for helping me find my own community. And, most important, thank you for always making me happy.

Spicy Potato Gratin

SERVES 10 TO 12

Have you ever tried crispy fries with chili crisp? If not, this is your sign to do that now. And, if you have, you know how potatoes, no matter how they are cooked, are the perfect vehicle to enjoy the spicy, dynamic flavors of chili crisp. I take the classic pairing of potatoes and chili crisp a step further in this rich, creamy, and cheesy gratin. There are three main reasons you should make this for your dinner party. First, the spicy, creamy sauce that binds the potatoes together proves that chili crisp and anything dairy belong together. Heavy cream and milk deliciously harmonize with spicy chili crisp so that both ingredients shine together. I would be happy just to toss cooked pasta in the sauce! Back to potatoes. Second, the stunning visual of stacking sliced potatoes vertically will certainly wow the crowd. Ever since I learned this technique from one of my culinary idols, Claire Saffitz, I've never gone back. It's also oddly satisfying to fill up a casserole with lines of stacked potatoes. And, lastly, this dish doesn't need to be served hot. It's even better when it's slightly cold or at room temperature, in my opinion. Right after it's baked, it might look like the sauce is broken because of the residual oil from the chili crisp, but the potatoes soak up that oil after a few minutes. Don't worry if it looks wrong at first; it will find its beauty after a few minutes of waiting. So, you can make it ahead, forget about it, and show off your potato art in a casserole for a crowd.

2 Tbsp unsalted butter, at room temperature

3 garlic cloves, minced (about 1 Tbsp)

1 shallot, finely diced

1 tsp all-purpose flour

1 cup [240 ml] milk

1 cup [240 ml] heavy cream

3 Tbsp chili crisp

½ cup [50 g] grated Gruyère cheese

1 Tbsp chopped thyme leaves

1½ tsp kosher salt

1 tsp freshly ground black pepper

3 lb [1.4 kg] russet potatoes, rinsed and scrubbed clean

¼ cup [40 g] grated Parmesan cheese

1 green onion, chopped, for garnish

1. Preheat the oven to 350°F [180°C].

2. In a medium sauté pan or skillet over low heat, melt 1 Tbsp of the butter. Add the minced garlic and diced shallot and cook for 1 to 2 minutes, or until fragrant. Add the flour to the pan to coat the garlic and shallots, and cook the mixture for a minute. Then pour in the milk and heavy cream while whisking to incorporate the garlic and shallots. Season the mixture with the chili crisp, grated Gruyère cheese, chopped thyme leaves, salt, and pepper. Increase the heat to medium-low and simmer until the sauce is slightly thickened but still runny, 8 to 10 minutes, stirring occasionally. Set aside.

3. Lightly grease all sides of an 8 by 8 in [20 by 20 cm] baking dish or casserole (6 cup [1.4 L] capacity) with the remaining 1 Tbsp of butter.

4. Thinly slice the potatoes, about ⅛ in [3 mm] thick, with the peel on, preferably using a mandoline. If you want, you can peel the potatoes, but keeping the skin on adds a nice texture when cooked.

cont'd.

Add a ladleful of the prepared cream sauce to the bottom of the dish. Then, arrange the potato slices vertically in the dish in overlapping rows, followed by a spoonful of sauce to coat the potatoes. Make sure each layer of stacked potatoes is touching the others. The cream sauce will hold the potatoes together, so add generous spoonful after each stack. Fill the dish by using smaller pieces of potato to fill in any gaps between stacks.

5. Pour the remaining chili crisp–cream mixture over the potatoes. Cover the dish with foil. Bake for 1 hour, or until all the potato slices are fork-tender.

6. When the potatoes are all cooked, remove the foil and sprinkle the grated Parmesan over the potatoes. Place it under the broiler, uncovered, for 2 to 3 minutes, or until the cheese is melted and the top is golden brown. Be sure to keep an eye on the dish to prevent burning.

7. Let it sit for at least 10 minutes before serving. Garnish with the green onions and serve. The leftovers can be stored in the fridge in an airtight container for up to 5 days.

Maple-Chili Roasted Carrots *with* Spicy Yogurt Sauce

Roasted carrots are simply magical. The carrots get slightly jammy and charred in some spots, and the hard flesh becomes pleasantly tender, making each bite irresistible. To turn up the volume on already magical roasted carrots, I added my chili crisp spin with a side of maple syrup. Chili crisp lends just the right amount of heat, while maple syrup takes the naturally sweet flavors of carrots to their full potential. But, the real hero of this dish is the spicy yogurt sauce. Greek yogurt takes a savory spin with minced garlic and bright lemon. Even though there's chili crisp in the spicy yogurt sauce, the creamy Greek yogurt mellows the heat and takes on a gorgeous grapefruit-like orange color. If roasted carrots are not your thing (I hope this recipe changes your mind!), you can give similar root vegetables like beets, parsnips, or even sweet potatoes the same roasted magic.

SERVES 2 OR 3

1½ lb [680 g] medium carrots, preferably rainbow carrots, halved lengthwise

3½ Tbsp chili crisp

2 Tbsp extra-virgin olive oil

3 tsp kosher salt

½ tsp freshly ground black pepper

1 Tbsp maple syrup

½ cup [120 g] full-fat Greek yogurt

3 Tbsp freshly squeezed lemon juice

1 Tbsp lemon zest

3 garlic cloves, minced (about 1 Tbsp)

1 tsp garlic powder

1 tsp rice wine vinegar

1 green onion, sliced lengthwise, for garnish

Toasted chopped pistachios, for garnish

Toasted sesame seeds, for garnish

1. Preheat the oven to 425°F [220°C]. Line a baking sheet with parchment paper.

2. Place the sliced carrots on the prepared baking sheet.

3. Whisk together 2 Tbsp of the chili crisp and the olive oil in a small bowl. Pour the chili crisp–olive oil dressing over the carrots and toss them to ensure they are well coated. Season the carrots with 1 tsp of the salt and the pepper.

4. Roast the carrots for 20 minutes, shaking the baking sheet halfway through. Remove the carrots from the oven and drizzle with the maple syrup. Toss the carrots again, preferably using tongs. Then, roast them in the oven for another 5 to 7 minutes, or until the carrots are deeply brown and fork-tender.

5. While the carrots are roasting, in a small bowl, combine the yogurt, lemon juice, lemon zest, remaining 1½ Tbsp of chili crisp, garlic, remaining 2 tsp of salt, garlic powder, and rice wine vinegar. Whisk to combine and set it aside.

6. Once the carrots are fully cooked, take them out of the oven. Smear the yogurt sauce on a serving plate, then arrange the roasted carrots on top using tongs. Garnish the dish with green onion, chopped pistachios, and toasted sesame seeds. Serve immediately. The leftovers can be stored in an airtight container in the fridge for up to 5 days.

Spicy, Lemony Charred Broccolini *with* Jammy Eggs

Two things make this charred broccolini dish extra special: spicy, lemony panko and jammy eggs with bright yolks. The bread crumbs are zippy and refreshing, thanks to lemon, with subtle heat from chili crisp. The jammy eggs' silky yolks add an element of richness. Charred broccolini gets slightly smoky and crispy outside, while the inside stays tender. Don't forget to shower it with a pile of grated Parmesan cheese at the end. It's a side dish that will steal the show from the main dish. Load it up with more jammy eggs, and serve it as a brunch dish with some toast.

SERVES 2 TO 4

3 large eggs

4 Tbsp [60 ml] extra-virgin olive oil

½ cup [30 g] panko

1 lemon

4 Tbsp [60 g] chili crisp

1 lb [455 g] broccolini, trimmed

Grated Parmesan cheese, for garnish

1. Bring a large pot of water to a boil, add the eggs, and cook for 6½ minutes. Fill a bowl with ice and water. Once the eggs are done, immediately transfer them to the ice-cold water to shock and stop the cooking. Keep them in cold water for 10 minutes while preparing the rest of the dish.

2. In a medium cast-iron skillet over medium-high heat, add 1 Tbsp of the olive oil and the panko. Lightly fry the bread crumbs until they turn golden brown, 3 to 5 minutes. Zest the lemon and reserve the zest. Cut the lemon in half. Save one half for garnish and squeeze the other half (roughly 2 Tbsp juice) over the bread crumbs and stir to combine. The lemon juice might initially make the bread crumbs soggy, but continue to cook for 30 to 60 seconds, or until they are crispy and no longer clumpy.

3. Transfer the bread crumbs to a medium bowl. Add the reserved lemon zest (about 1 tsp) and 2 Tbsp of the chili crisp. Mix to combine and set aside.

4. Halve any thick broccolini stems. Toss them with the remaining 3 Tbsp of olive oil.

5. Reheat the skillet over high heat for at least 2 minutes, or until smoking hot. Working in batches, add the broccolini to the hot pan and cook for 2 minutes, undisturbed, to get a nice char. Flip and cook for another 1 to 2 minutes, depending on how charred and crispy you want them.

Turn frequently after the intial charring process to evenly cook. The color of the broccolini should be darker green when it's done. Turn the heat to low, add the remaining chili crisp, and toss the seasoning with the charred vegetables.

6. When ready to assemble, peel the eggs. Arrange the charred vegetables on a serving platter and sprinkle with the bread crumbs. Halve the jammy eggs and place them around the platter. Squeeze the remaining lemon half over the broccolini, and finish the dish with showers of freshly grated Parmesan cheese. The leftovers can be stored in an airtight container in the fridge for up to 4 days.

Sausage Ya-Chae Bokkeum (Sausage *and* Vegetable Stir-Fry)

One of my favorite memories of growing up in Korea was eating my mom's simple dosirak, a so-called packaged meal in Korean. When I was in middle school, I asked her to pack me a dosirak for lunch every day because I hated going to the cafeteria. As a busy working mom, she didn't have much time to cook. Often, I gave her a list of easy, simple banchan (Korean side dishes) for my dosirak. And sausage ya-chae bokkeum was always my favorite. Short, Vienna-style sausages get slightly blistered in a hot pan and stir-fried with lots of crunchy vegetables like bell peppers and cabbage, all drenched in a sweet-and-salty, tangy sauce. My mom would make sausage ya-chae bokkeum as a part of my dosirak alongside kimchi, purple rice, and roasted seaweed. And, there was always a sweet message that said, "I love you, son! Have a good day!" written on a sticky note with her pretty handwriting. Sausage ya-chae bokkeum was a special banchan that she made to make me happy then, and I hope to one day make this upgraded, sweet-heat version for her with a note that says, "Thank you for being my mom!"

SERVES 2 TO 4

8 oz [230 g] Korean Vienna-style sausages or cocktail Frankfurt sausages

3 Tbsp chili crisp

1½ Tbsp ketchup

1 Tbsp oyster sauce

1½ tsp kosher salt

1 tsp honey

1 Tbsp neutral oil, such as vegetable or canola

1 yellow onion, sliced

2 green onions, chopped

2 garlic cloves, minced

2 cups [240 g] assorted chopped bell peppers

2 cups [120 g] chopped cabbage

Toasted sesame seeds, for garnish

Cooked rice, for serving

1. Give each sausage a few shallow, diagonal slits. This will help the sausage keep its shape and absorb the sauce better.

2. In a small bowl, mix together the chili crisp, ketchup, oyster sauce, salt, and honey to make the sauce. Set aside.

3. In a large skillet or sauté pan over medium-high heat, add the oil. Once the oil is hot, add the prepared sausages and cook for 2 to 3 minutes, or until the sides start to brown and create a nice crust.

4. Add the onion, green onions, and garlic to the pan and sauté for 1 to 2 minutes, or until fragrant. Then add the bell peppers and cabbage and cook for 2 to 4 minutes, or until the cabbage starts to wilt just a little. You want the vegetables to remain crisp rather than completely cooked.

5. Pour the prepared sauce into the pan and cook while stirring for 2 to 4 minutes, or until everything is thoroughly coated with the sauce.

6. Garnish with sprinkles of toasted sesame seeds. Serve it with rice or as a drinking snack with beer.

NOTE: This dish is fantastic as leftovers. You can keep it in an airtight container for up to 1 week in the fridge. You can reheat it in a microwave or on the stove in a pan with a bit of oil, but I love eating it cold, straight from the fridge with warm rice.

Spinach Namul *with* Fried Youtiao

Spinach namul is one of the easiest Korean banchan (side dishes) you can prepare. It starts with blanched spinach, mixed with nutty sauce, soy sauce, toasted sesame oil, and lots of crushed sesame seeds. It's simple yet tasty, and I can happily eat my feelings with just spinach namul and rice (and maybe Chili Crisp Fried Eggs [page 31] on top!). In my opinion, it's also one of the most beloved and commonly known Korean banchan to many people. On the other hand, youtiao, fried dough, is ubiquitous in Chinese cuisine. Because it's deep-fried, it has an insanely crunchy texture, often used in popular dishes like fan tuan, a Taiwanese rice roll, usually stuffed with pork floss but always with crispy youtiao. Thanks to chili crisp, these seemingly different dishes that represent their respective cultures come together. Chili crisp is used to season the blanched spinach, adding a surprise heat to the nutty, sesame-forward seasoning. Then, youtiao adds a unique crunch, a rare texture note to regular spinach namul. It's neither Korean nor Chinese, but the flavors, presentation, and textures have connections to both. This dish feels somewhat personal to me as I've been on this journey to create more chili crisp memories as a Korean immigrant. This new take on banchan captures the message of how a condiment can break the barriers of traditional flavors, creating something new yet familiar.

SERVES 2 OR 3

12 oz [340 g] baby spinach

2 green onions, chopped

2 garlic cloves, minced

1 Tbsp chili crisp

1 Tbsp toasted sesame oil

1 tsp soy sauce

½ tsp granulated sugar

½ tsp kosher salt

1 frozen, premade youtiao (Chinese fried dough), preferably Twin Marquis brand

1. Fill a large pot three-quarters full with water and bring to a boil over high heat.

2. Once the water boils, blanch the baby spinach for at least 40 seconds and no more than 1 minute. Drain the spinach in a colander and rinse it with running cold water. Using your hands, squeeze out as much excess water as you can. Repeat the process three or more times until there's no liquid coming out of the blanched spinach.

3. In a medium bowl, add the blanched spinach, green onions, garlic, chili crisp, sesame oil, soy sauce, sugar, and salt. Mix everything by hand to make sure all the spinach is coated with the seasonings. Set aside.

4. Cook the frozen, premade youtiao per the package directions until crispy. Cut into small pea-size pieces or crumbs.

5. Right before serving, add the chopped youtiao to the bowl with the seasoned spinach and mix everything with clean hands. Serve immediately. Spinach namul without youtiao can be stored in the fridge in an airtight container for up to 5 days. But, if spinach namul is already mixed with youtiao, I don't recommend storing leftovers because the youtaio will get soggy. Instead, cook youtiao separately and mix it with spinach namul right before serving.

Spicy Tofu *and* Broccoli Muchim

When I go out to eat at Korean restaurants, I always judge them by the quality of their banchan. They don't need to have a lot of options as long as they have a couple of solid choices that excite my appetite. I'm delighted when I see tofu and broccoli muchim as one of the banchan at Korean restaurants. *Muchim* means "mixed with seasonings" in Korean cuisine, and there are a variety of different muchim that often call for gochugaru, Korean red pepper flakes. But, tofu and broccoli muchim keeps things simple: just blanched broccoli mixed with tofu and a lot of sesame oil, which makes these two humble ingredients mouthwatering. Even though this is not a spicy dish, I always thought this beloved banchan would be even better with a little bit of heat, and chili crisp is a perfect addition. It adds a nice spice without overpowering the dish, and it doesn't compete with the toasty, nutty flavors of sesame oil. This dish is ideal to make ahead and keep in the fridge for the week or to eat as a light lunch salad, which I love to do.

SERVES 2 TO 4

1 ½ tsp kosher salt

8 oz [230 g] firm tofu

2 medium broccoli heads, trimmed and cut into bite-size pieces (you can include bite-size pieces of stems here)

2 Tbsp toasted sesame oil

2 Tbsp chili crisp

1 Tbsp soy sauce

1 tsp granulated sugar

2 garlic cloves, minced

1 green onion, chopped

1 Tbsp toasted sesame seeds

1. Fill a large pot with a lid three-quarters full with water and bring to a boil over medium-high heat. Once the water boils, add the salt. Add the tofu and cook it, covered, for 4 minutes, or until the tofu warms and softens. Carefully transfer the tofu with tongs or a slotted spoon to a small bowl and set aside.

2. In the same pot, cook the broccoli in the boiling water for 3 to 5 minutes, or until tender. Stir occasionally with a spatula or a wooden spoon to ensure all the florets are cooked.

3. Drain the broccoli in a colander and rinse with running cold water to keep its bright green color. Shake the broccoli in the colander a few times to get rid of excess moisture.

4. In a large bowl, add the cooked broccoli. Using a cheesecloth or kitchen towel, squeeze any excess moisture from the still-warm cooked tofu and add it to the bowl. Season it with the toasted sesame oil, chili crisp, soy sauce, sugar, garlic, and green onion. Mix everything with clean hands or gloves. Broken small tofu pieces should stick to the broccoli during mixing.

5. Sprinkle the toasted sesame seeds over the top and give everything a final mix before serving. Serve immediately, or store in an airtight container in the fridge for up to 5 days.

Limey Cantaloupe Salad *with* Chili Crisp–Fish Sauce Dressing

There's something so special about turning fresh fruit into a savory salad. When the sweet natural juice of the fruit is mixed with a savory dressing, it becomes an addictive yet refreshing bite. And this limey cantaloupe salad is a perfect example. Sweet, tender, and juicy cantaloupe chunks are tossed with a slightly spicy, addictively salty, and extra-zesty dressing. But what completes this salad is the topping. Chopped mint brightens the salad, while sliced almonds and thinly sliced onion add a flavorful crunch. Crumbled feta adds a tangy, salty, and creamy bite that's just the icing on the cake. If cantaloupe is not your favorite, try it with honeydew melon or watermelon. You will be surprised how well these naturally sweet, juicy, and crunchy fruits go with a salty, spicy dressing!

SERVES 2 TO 4

1 lb [455 g] cantaloupe, sliced into ¼ in [6 mm] triangular pieces

1 lime, zested and juiced

1 Tbsp extra-virgin olive oil

1½ tsp chili crisp, plus more for drizzling

1½ tsp fish sauce

1 tsp granulated sugar

¼ cup [10 g] chopped mint

½ red onion, thinly sliced

2 Tbsp sliced almonds

½ cup [60 g] crumbled feta

1. In a large bowl, add the cantaloupe, lime zest (about 2 tsp), and lime juice (about 2 Tbsp). Toss everything together.

2. In a small bowl, add the olive oil, chili crisp, fish sauce, and sugar. Whisk to combine.

3. Pour the dressing into the bowl with the cantaloupe and let it sit with the dressing for at least 5 minutes. Add the chopped mint and thinly sliced red onion. Toss everything to combine.

4. When ready to serve, garnish the salad with the sliced almonds, crumbled feta, and an extra drizzle of chili crisp. Serve immediately or keep it cold in the refrigerator until ready to serve. The leftovers can be stored in an airtight container in the refrigerator for up to 3 days.

NOTE: It's okay to have excess chili crisp–fish sauce dressing in the bowl. Think of it as quick marinating the sweet melon pieces in a tangy, salty sauce.

Chili Crisp Burrata Salad *with* Arugula, Apple, *and* Walnuts

I will be honest here: This salad is just an excuse for us to eat creamy burrata with chili crisp. And it's a fun performance for yourself or a crowd when cutting into a hunk of burrata drizzled with chili crisp. Every time I make this for a dinner party, my dinner guests go wild for it! The thrill and joy everyone gets from seeing the oil and bits of chili crisp fall into the crack of ooey, gooey burrata balls is simply marvelous. The creamy burrata balances the spicy chili crisp, creating a party of flavors that will make you roll your eyes with pleasure. Even though it's perfectly fine to eat just chili crisp–covered burrata, peppery arugula, and sweet apple bits make each bite of this salad exciting. The dressing also uses some chili crisp, which brings a pleasant warmth. When mixed with sweet, tart balsamic vinegar, it turns into an incredible vinaigrette for one of my favorite salads to eat all the time.

SERVES 4

1 Tbsp chili crisp, plus more for drizzling

1 ½ tsp extra-virgin olive oil

1 ½ tsp balsamic vinegar

Juice of ½ lemon (about 2 Tbsp)

1 tsp granulated sugar

9 oz [255 g] baby arugula

1 medium apple, such as Granny Smith or Honeycrisp, cored and diced

2 Tbsp roasted walnuts, chopped into small pieces

¼ cup [30 g] freshly grated Parmesan cheese

1 lb [455 g] burrata ball

Flaky sea salt

Freshly cracked black pepper

1. In a small bowl, add the chili crisp, olive oil, balsamic vinegar, lemon juice, and sugar. Whisk to combine.

2. In a large bowl, add the baby arugula, diced apple, and the dressing. Toss until everything is well coated with the dressing.

3. When ready to serve, place the dressed arugula on a platter. Scatter the chopped walnuts over the top and sprinkle with the Parmesan.

4. Place the burrata ball in the center of the platter and drizzle with extra chili crisp right on top. Sprinkle with flaky sea salt and freshly cracked black pepper and serve.

NOTE: It's best to grate Parmesan on top of the salad before serving, using a Microplane rather than pregrated Parmesan cheese.

Spicy Green Onion Pancakes (Pa-Jeon)

I love green onions in all forms, especially in crispy, savory pancakes, called jeon in Korean cuisine. Compared to Chinese green onion pancakes, which are flakier and doughier, Korean green onion pancakes use liquid batter to create crisp edges with a more green onion–forward taste. Tapioca flour is key to creating the shatteringly crunchy texture, which almost resembles fried chicken. Loads of green onions lightly coated with the liquid batter, rather than enveloped in a dough, lets you taste the ultimate, savory flavors of fried green onions. And chili crisp adds just enough heat to harmonize with the oniony flavors in the pancake. These deliciously greasy and crunchy pancakes pair fantastically with any alcohol, especially ice-cold beer or makgeolli, Korean rice wine.

MAKES THREE OR FOUR 4 IN [10 CM] PANCAKES

½ cup [70 g] all-purpose flour

½ cup [75 g] tapioca flour

2 large eggs

2 Tbsp chili crisp, plus more for garnish

1 tsp soy sauce

1 onion, sliced

6 or 7 green onions, cut into 3 to 4 in [7.5 to 10 cm] lengths

¼ cup [60 ml] neutral oil, such as vegetable or canola, or more for frying

Kosher salt, for sprinkling

1. In a small bowl, whisk together the all-purpose flour, tapioca flour, eggs, chili crisp, soy sauce, and ⅓ cup [80 ml] of water. The batter should resemble a thick pancake batter. Once the batter is ready, add the sliced onion and green onion pieces. Make sure all the pieces are well coated in the batter. No need to rest the batter here.

2. In a medium skillet or sauté pan, heat the oil over medium-high heat. It might seem like a lot of oil, but there should be enough to shallow-fry the batter. Depending on the pan size, if it's not enough oil to create a puddle in the pan, add more. Once the oil is hot, add about ⅓ cup [70 g] of the mixed batter to the pan. Press it down with the bottom of a spoon or a spatula to flatten out the pancake. Cook for 4 to 6 minutes, or until the edges are crisp and brown. Carefully flip and cook for another 2 to 3 minutes, or until the batter is no longer liquidy. Repeat the process with the remaining pancake batter.

3. As soon as the pancakes are done, transfer them to a serving plate and sprinkle with a pinch of salt.

4. Serve while they are hot with an extra dollop of chili crisp on top. The leftover pancakes can be frozen. Reheat in a 400°F [200°C] oven for 8 to 10 minutes, flipping midway when they start sizzling, until the pancakes are warm. If you have an air fryer, which is the best reheating tool for frozen items in my opinion, air-fry at 350°F [180°C] for 3 to 5 minutes, or until the pancakes are toasty outside.

chapter 5

DESSERTS WITH A TWIST

SAVORY DESSERTS ARE HERE TO STAY

Spicy desserts are nothing new, but still, chili crisp on desserts is something that turns off many people. In fact, it turned me off too at first. I tested the Spicy Peach and Mixed Berry Crumble (page 160) using one of my go-to chili crisps, Lao Gan Ma. At first, everything seemed fine. Peaches, coated with chili flakes, even looked delicious after they came out of the oven. I took a bite of it, and there was something off that didn't quite impress me. Maybe I needed to make adjustments to the ratio. I started thinking of how I could transform this "meh" dessert into "WOW."

I took a bite of it the next day, and that's when I was truly shocked. The garlicky, oniony, extreme umami taste of Lao Gan Ma Spicy Chili Crisp was beyond aggressive. Just think about cooked, soft peaches with an intense garlic flavor. Yeah, it was a traumatic experience. And I started to reproach myself. I couldn't possibly let people taste what I tasted. I almost felt betrayed by my favorite chili crisp, which truly went well with everything, including ice cream. So, I started to think hard: How could I turn around this defeating moment?

As a solution, I developed a chili crisp specific to baked desserts: just chili flakes, oil, sugar, and salt. No fried shallots, garlic, green onions, or any of the savory components that really make chili crisp satisfying. Instead, I decided to add an assortment of nuts, which lends a nice texture, especially in baked goods. And that's how my Very Nutty Chili Crisp (page 19) was created specifically for desserts.

Even though this particular chili crisp is designed to be paired with desserts, its simple list of ingredients creates pure, clean, spicy flavors that go with everything, including all things savory. And, hoping that I wouldn't taste garlicky warm peaches again, I made Spicy Peach and Mixed Berry Crumble (page 160) again with my Very Nutty Chili Crisp (page 19), and it was absolutely fantastic. Sweet, jammy juice from cooked peaches and berries gets slightly elevated with the spice from chili crisp without any overpowering savory taste. It tasted just like classic crumbles, but in about 5 seconds, a pleasant wave of spice comes through as a delicious surprise. My Very Nutty Chili Crisp transformed my garlicky peach nightmare into a spicy daydream.

You can use different types of chili crisp if you feel adventurous and curious, but I highly encourage you to use only Very Nutty Chili Crisp for making recipes in the dessert chapter. But if you want to taste garlic in your dessert, go ahead, I won't judge.

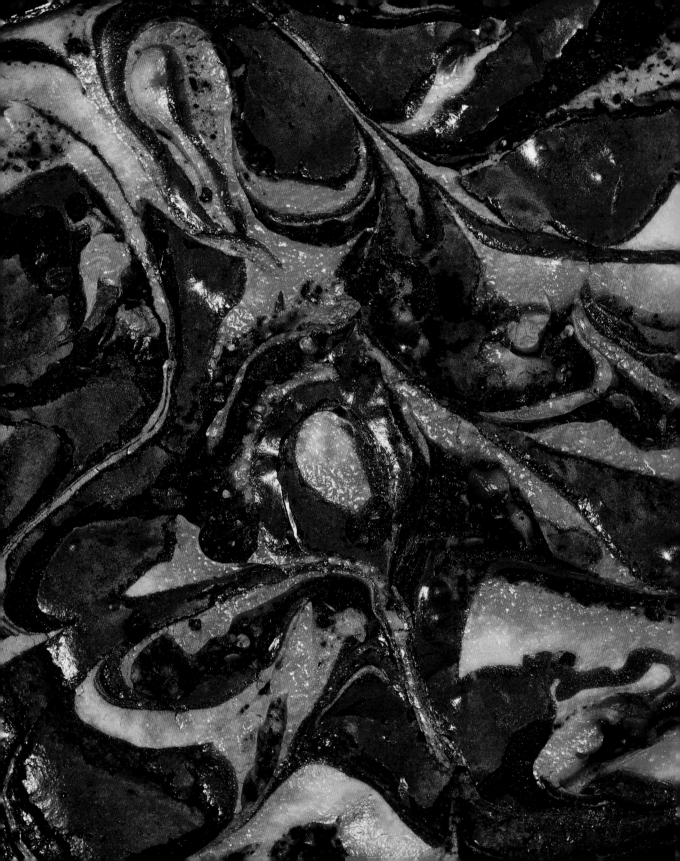

Spicy Tahini Cream Cheese Swirled Brownies

MAKES 9 TO 16 SQUARES

BROWNIE BATTER

One 18 oz [500 g] box brownie mix, plus any additional ingredients per package instructions

3 Tbsp Very Nutty Chili Crisp (page 19)

1 tsp kosher salt

TAHINI–CREAM CHEESE LAYER

8 oz [230 g] cream cheese

¼ cup [50 g] granulated sugar

2 Tbsp tahini

1 large egg

1 tsp vanilla extract

CHILI CRISP AND BATTER SWIRL

1 Tbsp Very Nutty Chili Crisp (page 19)

I've never made brownies from scratch because I think boxed brownies are perfect the way they are. It's magical how you need to add only oil, egg, or sometimes just water to make a delicious brownie. Humble boxed brownies can turn into a stunning dessert with a few extra elements, like a tahini–cream cheese layer and chili crisp swirls. Tahini adds an extra nuttiness to the sweet cream cheese. And the cream cheese layer becomes a beautiful canvas to channel your inner artist with swirls. This recipe will surprise you with what your typical boxed brownie mix can become!

1. Preheat the oven to the temperature indicated on the package directions. Butter a 9 in [23 cm] square baking pan and line it with parchment paper.

2. **To make the brownie batter:** Prepare your brownie batter according to the package directions. Once the batter is made, add the chili crisp and salt. Mix everything together. Set aside 1 Tbsp of the batter for the swirl on top later. Pour the remaining batter into your prepared baking pan.

3. **To make the tahini–cream cheese layer:** In a food processor, add the cream cheese, sugar, tahini, egg, and vanilla and run the processor until everything is smooth.

4. Pour the tahini–cream cheese layer on top of the brownies in the baking pan. Spread it across the pan to make sure it covers the brownie batter, then set the pan aside.

5. **To make the chili crisp and batter swirl:** In a small bowl, add ½ tsp of water to the reserved batter to make it a little loose. With a spoon, add small dollops of chili crisp across the tahini–cream cheese layer, followed by dollops of brownie batter. Using a chopstick or something similar, make swirls through the chili crisp and brownie batter dollops.

6. Bake the brownies according to the package directions. Let them cool slightly and serve warm. The brownies can be stored in an airtight container at room temperature for up to 4 days.

Spicy Coconut Mochi Bites

Mochi is one of my favorite treats. Its chewy, bouncy texture is an absolute delight to eat. These coconut mochi bites have a ton of creamy, spicy flavors from the coconut milk and chili crisp. It's mesmerizing to see how white coconut milk turns a deep orange color that reminds me of a maple leaf with specks of chili flakes. The coconut flavor comes through in three separate layers: batter, glaze, and coconut flakes on top—each adding a different, deeper level of coconut to this soft, chewy dessert. I love the flavor pairing of coconut and chili crisp, but if coconut flavor doesn't spark joy, you can replace it with regular milk or even heavy cream. There is a phrase in Korean eating culture called "mouth is bored," which refers to the moments when you are not hungry per se, but you want a little bite to feel satisfied. Taking a bite of this creamy, spicy dessert is pure happiness, and I love it as a late-night snack as I'm getting comfy with a Korean drama on TV.

MAKES 16 SQUARES

2 cups [280 g] glutinous rice flour or mochiko flour (see Note)

1 cup [200 g] granulated sugar

2 tsp baking powder

1 ½ tsp kosher salt

One 13 ½ oz [400 ml] can full-fat coconut milk

2 large eggs

3 Tbsp Very Nutty Chili Crisp (page 19)

2 Tbsp vanilla extract

⅓ cup [40 g] confectioners' sugar

½ cup [40 g] unsweetened shredded coconut flakes

1. Preheat the oven to 350°F [180°C]. Line a 9 in [23 cm] square baking pan with parchment paper.

2. In a large bowl, combine the rice flour, granulated sugar, baking powder, and salt. Mix to combine.

3. Open the canned coconut milk and reserve 2 Tbsp for later. In a separate medium bowl, add the eggs, chili crisp, vanilla, and the rest of the coconut milk and whisk to combine.

4. Pour the wet mixture into the dry mixture. Mix everything until the batter is smooth with no lumps.

5. Transfer the batter to the prepared baking pan.

6. Bake for 45 to 50 minutes, or until a tester inserted into the center comes out clean. Let it cool in the pan for at least 15 minutes, or until the baking pan isn't hot anymore.

7. While the mochi bakes, in a small bowl, whisk the confectioners' sugar and the reserved 2 Tbsp of coconut milk to combine.

8. When the mochi is slightly cool, pour the glaze on top of the mochi in the pan. Spread it evenly so that it drips down the sides of the mochi. Immediately sprinkle the shredded coconut flakes on top so that they stick to the glaze. Let the mochi soak in the glaze for at least 10 minutes.

9. Take the baked mochi out of the baking pan. Slice it into sixteen small squares. Serve warm. The mochi bites can be stored in an airtight container at room temperature for up to 3 days.

NOTE: Be sure to use glutinous rice flour, not regular rice flour, because regular rice flour doesn't create a chewy bite when baked.

Sesame-Crusted Gochugaru Shortbread Cookies

When I was in a culinary school, there was an annual cookie competition where students showcased their brilliant cookie recipes. Even though it was mostly for pastry students, there were a few culinary students, and I was one of them. At that time, I was going through a phase of making shortbread cookies, and I submitted my honey–butter–potato chip shortbread cookies, representing the flavors of Korea. It was a completely different approach compared to the rest of the contestants. Even though I was proud to present my not-sugar-forward cookies, the judges seemed confused. One French pastry chef even mocked my cookies for tasting so salty, "like the ocean." My untraditional shortbread cookies might not have won, but I was still proud of them for pushing the boundaries of what cookies could be.

This sesame-crusted gochguaru cookie is a spicy, leveled-up version of those shortbreads. The combination of fruity yet deeply savory gochugaru and chili crisp gives the cookies a pleasant warmth. The secret ingredient that makes it extra special is rosemary, which brings its lemony-pine flavors as a kicker. And it's so easy: Just dump all the ingredients in a food processor, and you are pretty much done. Here's a message to the French chef who couldn't stop talking about how weird my cookies were: You can make spicy cookies with chili crisp and chili flakes, and they are incredibly delicious.

MAKES 24 TO 28 COOKIES

2 cups [280 g] all-purpose flour

²⁄₃ cup [130 g] granulated sugar

1 tsp kosher salt

2 Tbsp Very Nutty Chili Crisp (page 19)

1 Tbsp gochugaru

1 Tbsp chopped fresh rosemary

1 cup [226 g] cold salted butter, chopped

¼ cup [35 g] black sesame seeds

¼ cup [35 g] toasted white sesame seeds

1. In the food processor, add the flour, sugar, salt, chili crisp, gochugaru, and rosemary. Pulse a few times to mix everything well. Add the butter and pulse until the dough comes together.

2. In a small bowl, mix the black sesame seeds and toasted white sesame seeds. Set them aside.

3. Divide the dough in half. Prepare a long piece of plastic wrap for each half. Spread half of the mixed sesame seeds on a piece of plastic wrap, then place half of the dough on top of the seeds. Fold the plastic over to cover the dough with the sesame seeds.

4. Using the plastic wrap as a guide, roll the dough on a flat surface and shape it into a log 2 in [5 cm] in diameter, massaging it so it doesn't have any holes or gaps. The sesame seeds will be mixed into the dough slightly during the process, which is okay. Repeat the same process for the other half. Chill the dough logs in the fridge until firm, at least

cont'd.

1 hour. If you need to quickly chill the dough, you can put it in the freezer for 30 minutes.

5. Preheat the oven to 350°F [180°C] and line a baking sheet with parchment paper.

6. When the logs are chilled and very firm to the touch, unwrap the dough from the plastic. Slice each log into ½ in [13 mm] thick rounds. Each log should yield 12 to 14 cookies.

7. Put the sliced rounds on the prepared baking sheet about 1 in [2.5 cm] apart. Bake them for 15 to 17 minutes, or until the edges are slightly brown and the tops are soft to the touch.

8. Let cool for at least 15 minutes before serving. The cookies can be stored at room temperature in an airtight container for up to 5 days.

NOTE: You can make the cookie dough logs in advance and keep them in the freezer for up to 3 months. When ready to bake, let the logs thaw for a few minutes, then slice into thick rounds. Bake and enjoy!

Fluffy Chocolate Roll Cake *with* Strawberry Chili Crisp

One of my favorite childhood items at the bakery was a roll cake. Even though I was never a cake person, there was something so enticing about fluffy sponge cake, beautifully rolled with whipped cream. I didn't think it was something that I could ever make, but this was one of the dishes that I had to perfect as part of an assignment when I was in culinary school. I must say, the shape didn't always turn out as perfectly swirled as I hoped. But, after making so many roll cakes, I realized that as long as I could get a bite of the cake and whipped cream together, it would still taste good no matter how pretty (or not) it looked. And this chocolate roll cake proves that. The cake itself is light and airy, thanks to the meringue incorporated into the batter. And chili crisp comes through very subtly as a pleasant surprise because of the dominant chocolate flavor. The filling, which makes this roll cake extra special, is the definition of sweet and spicy.

When you roll the cake, I highly suggest adding dollops of the strawberry jelly–chili crisp mixture on top of the whipped cream rather than mixing it in. This method lets the white whipped cream layer stand out as a clear contrast to the chocolate cake while allowing pockets of sweet-and-spicy flavors to surprise in each bite. Making a roll cake might be daunting and a somewhat time-consuming task at first. But it will be so worth it once you take a bite of this flavor combo. If you don't want to go through the exciting journey of making the roll cake from scratch, you can make the strawberry jelly–chili crisp mixture and put dollops on your toast. It's a quick way to taste something different yet so familiar.

ROLL CAKE

4 large eggs

1 cup [200 g] granulated sugar

½ cup [70 g] all-purpose flour

3 Tbsp cocoa powder

FILLING

1 cup [240 ml] heavy cream

3 Tbsp strawberry jelly

2 Tbsp Very Nutty Chili Crisp (page 19)

GANACHE

½ cup [120 ml] heavy cream

2 Tbsp unsalted butter

½ cup [90 g] semisweet chocolate chips

2 Tbsp Very Nutty Chili Crisp (page 19)

GARNISHES

Confectioners' sugar, for dusting

Fresh strawberries, sliced

1. Preheat the oven to 375°F [190°C]. Line a half-sheet pan with parchment paper. Set it aside.

2. **To make the roll cake:** Separate the eggs and place the yolks in a medium bowl and the whites in the bowl of a stand mixer. If using a handheld mixer, add the whites to a separate large bowl.

3. Add ½ cup [100 g] of the granulated sugar to the bowl with the yolks. Using a whisk, beat them together until the mixture is pale and thick enough to hold a ribbon for a few minutes. Set it aside.

cont'd.

4. In a separate bowl, sift the flour and cocoa powder. Set it aside.

5. Slowly whip the egg whites. When they hold very soft peaks, after about a minute, add the remaining ½ cup [100 g] of granulated sugar to the bowl. Continue to beat, while increasing the speed to medium, until the meringue is stiff but not dry, about 4 minutes.

6. Pour the egg yolk–sugar mixture into the meringue and gently fold in using a silicone spatula. Gradually add the flour-cocoa mixture while folding the egg mixtures together. Do this gently and quickly until everything is thoroughly mixed in.

7. Pour the batter into the prepared half-sheet pan and spread out with a spatula, making sure the batter covers all the corners. Tap the half-sheet pan a few times on the counter to remove any air bubbles.

8. Bake the cake for 13 to 15 minutes, or until the cake springs back when touched in the middle.

9. Once the cake is done baking, take it out of the oven and cover it with a damp towel. Let it cool for at least 5 minutes. Then, invert the cake onto the damp towel by flipping the pan. Remove the parchment paper from the cake.

10. While keeping the damp towel on the bottom, roll up the cake and the towel lengthwise, as if you are rolling a cigar, then let it cool, preferably in the fridge. When rolling, the damp towel should create a barrier so that the cake doesn't stick to each other. This process is crucial when making a roll cake because it helps train the cake into the roll shape.

11. **While the rolled cake is cooling, make the filling:** In a stand mixer or in a large bowl with a handheld mixer, whip the heavy cream until it has firm peaks, 7 to 8 minutes.

12. In a small bowl, mix the jelly and chili crisp to combine. Set it aside.

13. When the cake is completely cooled, unroll it on fresh parchment paper. Spread the whipped cream layer over the cake first, then add dollops of strawberry jelly–chili crisp mixture on top.

14. Starting from the edge, fold the rim in and begin to roll the cake up tightly. Use the parchment paper to shape and hold the cake tight to prevent any gaps while rolling. The roll should be tight, and if any dollops of strawberry jelly–chili crisp squeeze out, it's totally fine.

15. Cool the rolled cake in the refrigerator for at least 30 minutes so that the fillings firm up.

16. **While the cake cools, prepare the ganache:** In a microwave-safe medium bowl, add the heavy cream and butter. Microwave for 1 minute, or until the butter is completely melted and the heavy cream is hot. If it's not hot, continue microwaving in increments of 15 seconds. Add the chocolate chips and chili crisp to the hot cream mixture and whisk gently until the mixture comes together and turns glossy. Set it aside.

17. After at least 30 minutes in the refrigerator, place the cooled cake on a wire cooling rack over a sheet pan. Pour the warm ganache over the roll cake and spread it with a spatula to even it out. Make sure the ganache covers the surface completely from end to end.

18. Return the roll cake to the refrigerator until the ganache firms up, about 30 minutes. When ready to serve, dust with confectioners' sugar and garnish with slices of fresh strawberries. Cut it with a warm knife. The leftovers can be stored in an airtight container in the refrigerator for 3 to 4 days.

Spicy Citrus Pound Cake

Chili crisp? In a cake?! That was many of my friends' first reaction when I presented this delightfully zesty treat. When they took a bite of it they said, "I don't taste much of the spice?" And, funny enough, about 5 seconds later, everyone said, "Oh, wait a minute! I taste the chili crisp!"

That's the beauty of this bright treat. The moist, citrus flavors from the lemon and orange greet you immediately. Then, the lovely, warming flavors of chili crisp arrive, as if they are the late VIP guests. I love the balance of lemon and orange in this recipe, but you can use any type of citrus. One trick to making a flavorful pound cake is to make a syrup coat with citrus zest and freshly squeezed juice, a delicious tip I learned from watching Ina Garten! This sweet-and-bright syrup coat creates a layer between the cake and the glaze, which both have chili crisp.

This recipe proves how citrus and heat go hand in hand. The flavor combination is truly incredible!

1. Preheat the oven to 325°F [170°C]. Spray a 9 by 5 in [23 by 13 cm] loaf pan with nonstick cooking spray and line it with parchment paper so that the paper hangs off the two long sides to make it easier to remove the cake after it's baked.

2. **To make the cake:** In a large bowl, whisk together the flour, brown sugar, salt, baking powder, and baking soda.

3. In a medium bowl, add the sour cream, eggs, vegetable oil, chili crisp, orange zest, orange juice, lemon zest, lemon juice, and vanilla. Whisk to combine.

4. Add the wet mixture to the dry mixture. Whisk until everything is thoroughly mixed and the batter is smooth.

5. Pour the batter into the prepared loaf pan and smooth the top with a spatula. Bake for 50 to 60 minutes, or until the top is lightly browned and a toothpick inserted in the center comes out clean. Check every 5 minutes after an hour in the oven.

cont'd.

MAKES ONE 9 BY 5 IN [23 BY 13 CM] POUND CAKE

CAKE

1⅓ cups [185 g] all-purpose flour

¾ cup [150 g] light brown sugar

1 tsp kosher salt

½ tsp baking powder

¼ tsp baking soda

1 cup [240 g] sour cream

3 large eggs

⅓ cup [80 ml] vegetable oil

3 Tbsp Very Nutty Chili Crisp (page 19)

2 tsp orange zest

2 Tbsp freshly squeezed orange juice

2 tsp lemon zest

1 Tbsp freshly squeezed lemon juice

1 tsp vanilla extract

CITRUS SYRUP COAT

¼ cup [50 g] granulated sugar

1 tsp lemon zest

1 tsp orange zest

2 Tbsp fresh lemon juice

2 Tbsp fresh orange juice

cont'd.

6. **While the cake is baking, make the citrus syrup coat:** In a small saucepan over medium-low heat, combine the granulated sugar, lemon zest, orange zest, lemon juice, and orange juice and let cook for a few minutes, or until the sugar is fully dissolved and starts to thicken like a syrup. When the cake is done baking, let it cool slightly for 5 minutes, then pour the syrup over the cake in the pan. Let the cake cool completely before glazing, 20 to 25 minutes.

7. **To make the glaze:** In a medium bowl, combine the confectioners' sugar, lemon juice, orange juice, lemon zest, orange zest, and chili crisp and mix thoroughly.

8. Once the cake is completely cooled, dust the top with extra confectioner's sugar to coat, then drizzle with the thin glaze back and forth all over the cake. The cake can be tightly wrapped and kept at room temperature for up to 4 days.

GLAZE

½ cup [60 g] confectioners' sugar, plus more for dusting

1 ½ tsp freshly squeezed lemon juice

1 ½ tsp freshly squeezed orange juice

2 tsp lemon zest

2 tsp orange zest

1 ½ tsp Very Nutty Chili Crisp (page 19)

Spicy Peach *and* Mixed Berry Crumble

I am a big frozen fruit stan. I have a cup of frozen fruit almost every day as a midday snack. The texture might not be as juicy as fresh fruit, but there's something cooling (literally!) and satisfying about enjoying frozen fruit at ease. As a big lover of crumbles, I always make them with frozen fruit. And, the best part? You don't have to defrost the fruit at all. Of course, at the peak of summer, when peaches and berries are so juicy and flavorful, you can use them straight from the farmers' market, but I don't have those kinds of luxuries all the time, okay?! Store-bought frozen fruit is just fine and equally delicious.

This is a pretty classic recipe with two twists: the addition of chili crisp and the technique of grating butter. Spicy chili crisp works beautifully with berries and peaches, and the sweetness of the fruit mellows down the spice. Using grated butter creates extra-flaky crumbles, a nicely satisfying topping for the jammy fruit. If you are skeptical about using frozen fruit, give this recipe a try. You won't know the difference, especially after it's cooked down. The juice from the frozen fruit still gets deliciously jammy with a nice kick. If you use fresh fruit, just halve the amount of starch called for in the recipe (or completely omit it if you like it less jammy) and check it after 30 minutes of baking because fresh fruit doesn't need as much time to cook down. It will be a spicy way to appreciate your luxurious fresh fruit. I should treat myself to fresh fruit sometime, right? But, until then, I will continue using my reliable frozen fruits.

Oh, one last thing: Serving this with ice cream is not just an option. It's a MUST. And yes, put another drizzle of chili crisp on top of the ice cream.

SERVES 6 TO 8

FRUIT FILLING

2 lb [910 g] frozen peaches

1 lb [455 g] frozen mixed berries

⅔ cup [130 g] light brown sugar

1 lemon, zested and juiced

¼ cup [45 g] potato starch or cornstarch

¼ cup [60 g] Very Nutty Chili Crisp (page 19), plus more for drizzling

CRUMBLES

1 cup [140 g] all-purpose flour

⅓ cup [65 g] granulated sugar

1 tsp kosher salt

1 tsp baking powder

½ tsp ground cinnamon

1 tsp vanilla extract

½ cup [113 g] cold salted butter

Ice cream or whipped cream, for serving

1. Preheat the oven to 375°F [190°C].

2. **To make the fruit filling:** Thaw the frozen fruit for a few minutes, or until they are no longer frozen and stuck together.

3. In a large bowl, add the slightly thawed peaches and berries, brown sugar, lemon zest (about 1 Tbsp), lemon juice (about 2 Tbsp), potato starch, and chili crisp. Toss everything to make sure all the fruit is coated. If the frozen fruit creates any clumps, be sure to break them apart. Let sit for 5 to 10 minutes while you prepare the crumbles.

4. **To make the crumbles:** In a separate bowl, add the flour, granulated sugar, salt, baking powder, cinnamon, and vanilla. Then, using either a Microplane or the small holes of a grater, grate the cold butter directly into the bowl of dry ingredients. With clean hands, rub the grated butter into the dry ingredients. There should be some clumps here and there, and the mixture should resemble bread crumbs.

5. In a 9 by 13 in [23 by 33 cm] baking pan or a 12 in [30 cm] cast-iron pan, add the dressed-up fruit. Spread it out into an even layer. Sprinkle the crumbles all over the fruit, being sure to leave big clumps here and there for texture. Bake for 45 to 50 minutes, or until the top of the crumbles is toasted and golden brown and the fruit juices around the edges are jammy.

6. Serve warm, with a scoop of vanilla ice cream or a dollop of whipped cream with an extra drizzle of chili crisp on top. The leftovers can be stored in an airtight container in the refrigerator for 2 to 3 days. Reheat it as necessary in the oven or microwave.

Spicy
Lemony Ice
Cream
(page 163)

Spicy Vanilla
Ice Cream with
Chocolate
Shavings
(page 164)

Chili Crisp Ice Cream Two Ways

If you love chili crisp as much as I do, adding a drizzle of it on top of ice cream is not that wild of an idea. I love this combo because creamy vanilla ice cream harmonizes with the flavors of chili crisp beautifully. I took this classic combo a step further by mixing chili crisp into the ice cream base. And the result was something astonishing!

I used my go-to no-churn ice cream as a base because who has an ice cream machine at home, right? If you do, I envy you! The simple combination of condensed milk and cold heavy cream creates a luscious, slightly fudgy texture that tastes as good and fresh as a scoop from your favorite ice cream shop. It's mesmerizing to see the ice cream turn a gorgeous apricot color as you mix in chili crisp and condensed milk. It's fascinating to see chili flakes speckled throughout the custard, and once you take a bite, the pleasant flavors will be engraved in your palate for good.

I made two different flavor suggestions for this chili crisp ice cream base. One leans into zesty, bright lemon flavors, which complements the spice. The other is a classic vanilla-chocolate combo, which tames the spice slightly. I think the lemony flavor would be fantastic to serve after something rich and hearty, like grilled steak, while the vanilla-chocolate would be a memorable way to finish a homey dinner like roasted chicken. And here's a tip: Make Sesame-Crusted Gochugaru Shortbread Cookies (page 153), crumble them into big pieces, and sprinkle them on top of the ice cream to add texture. It's a fantastic duo.

Spicy Lemony Ice Cream

SERVES 4 TO 6

1. In a large bowl, add the condensed milk, lemon juice (about ¼ cup [60 ml]), lemon zest (about 1 Tbsp), chili crisp, and vanilla. Mix to combine.

2. Put the cream in a medium bowl. Using an electric hand mixer, beat the cream until stiff peaks form, 3 to 4 minutes. Alternatively, use a food processor to make whipped cream. Pour the cold cream into the bowl of the food processor bowl and run for 2 minutes, or until stiff peaks form.

3. Fold the whipped cream into the condensed milk mixture with a large spatula until everything is well mixed.

4. Use a spatula to transfer the ice cream base to a freezer-safe container with a lid and smooth the top. If you like, you can lay a piece of parchment paper directly on top of the ice cream base to prevent any ice crystals from forming.

5. Freeze for at least 6 hours before serving. The ice cream tastes best when eaten within 2 weeks of making.

cont'd.

One 14 oz [400 g] can sweetened condensed milk

1 large lemon, zested and juiced

3 Tbsp Very Nutty Chili Crisp (page 19)

1 tsp vanilla extract

2 cups [480 ml] cold heavy cream

Spicy Vanilla Ice Cream *with* Chocolate Shavings

1. In a large bowl, add the condensed milk, vanilla, and chili crisp. Mix to combine.

2. Put the cream in a medium bowl. Using an electric hand mixer, beat the cream until stiff peaks form, 3 to 4 minutes. Alternatively, use a food processor to make whipped cream. Pour the cold cream into the bowl of a food processor and run for 2 minutes, or until stiff peaks form.

3. Fold the whipped cream into the condensed milk mixture with a large spatula until everything is well mixed.

4. Using a vegetable peeler or a Microplane, shave the chocolate bar until you get about ½ cup [45 g] or more. Fold the chocolate shavings into the ice cream mixture.

The chocolate shavings are supposed to be broken into little pieces; if you see any big chunks of chocolate, be sure to break them apart. By doing so, the chocolate shavings won't freeze too much as the ice cream base solidifies.

5. Use a spatula to transfer the ice cream base to a freezer-safe container with a lid and smooth the top. If you like, you can lay a piece of parchment paper directly on top of the ice cream base to prevent any ice crystals from forming.

6. Freeze for at least 6 hours before serving. The ice cream tastes best when eaten within 2 weeks of making. Serve it with extra shavings of chocolate on top.

SERVES 4 TO 6

One 14 oz [400 g] can sweetened condensed milk

3 Tbsp vanilla extract

3 Tbsp Very Nutty Chili Crisp (page 19)

2 cups [480 ml] cold heavy cream

1¾ oz [50 g] dark chocolate bar

Spiced Sweet Potato Basque Cheesecake

MAKES ONE 6 IN [15 CM] CAKE

8 oz [230 g] cream cheese

½ cup [100 g] granulated sugar

1 cup [200 g] cooked, roasted sweet potatoes (see Note)

2 Tbsp sweet potato starch, tapioca starch, or cornstarch

½ cup [120 ml] heavy cream

¼ cup [60 ml] maple syrup

2 Tbsp Very Nutty Chili Crisp (page 19)

2 large eggs

If there's one thing you should know about me, besides being your chili crisp hype man, I'm an air fryer fanatic. Originally I thought it was just another piece of cooking equipment that would take up space in my kitchen. But it's not an understatement to say that the air fryer has completely transformed my life for good. Out of the many recipes I've tried in my air fryer, this basque cheesecake has brought me more joy than I ever thought possible from a piece of equipment.

Basque cheesecake, the so-called burnt cheesecake, has a distinctively different look from a classic cheesecake because of its deep-brown top. Inside is an ooey, gooey, fudgy, creamy cheesecake that tastes like a cloud made of cream cheese. Once again, chili crisp and anything dairy are best friends, so of course it was inevitable for me to experiment.

This spiced sweet potato basque cheesecake tastes like the comfort of Thanksgiving side dishes. There's a little bit of earthiness from cooked sweet potatoes. A fabulous hint of maple syrup and chili crisp come after. Then, the wonderful texture of the heavy cream and cream cheese makes this dessert decadent and indulgent. It's almost ridiculous how easy it is to make: Dump all the ingredients, blend, pour, bake, and you're done! Using an air fryer for baking, rather than the oven, guarantees the gorgeous deep-brown top. If you've been hesitant to get an air fryer, let this recipe be the reason you finally do. You won't regret it!

1. Preheat the air fryer to 400°F [200°C] for 5 minutes. If using the oven, preheat it to 425°F [220°C]. Line a 6 in [15 cm] round cake pan, preferably with a removable bottom, with parchment paper. Set it aside.

2. In a blender, add the cream cheese, sugar, sweet potatoes, sweet potato starch, cream, maple syrup, chili crisp, and eggs. Blend until the mixture is smooth. It should be thick yet runny, almost like a milkshake. Pour the cake batter into the prepared cake pan.

3. Air fryer method: Place the pan in the preheated air fryer and bake for 10 minutes. Then lower the temperature to 350°F [180°C] for 16 minutes. If you prefer the cheesecake to be firmer inside, add 2 to 4 minutes more. When pulled out of the air fryer, the cake mixture should still be jiggly.

4. Oven method: Bake for 35 to 40 minutes, or until the top looks almost burnt. If the top isn't browning, turn on the broiler for a minute, or until the cake takes on the desired color. The cheesecake will be jiggly in the pan.

cont'd.

5. Let cool to room temperature, then refrigerate, uncovered, for at least 6 hours, preferably overnight, before slicing. Serve cold. The leftovers can be stored in the fridge for up to 1 week.

NOTE: To get the best flavor from the sweet potatoes, bake them in the oven. Stab the sweet potatoes all around with a fork, then bake them at 450°F [230°C] for 45 minutes to 1 hour, or until the natural sugars from the sweet potatoes seep out from the fork holes. Let them cool completely, then scoop out the flesh.

Experiment with different types of sweet potatoes in this recipe! Each sweet potato has different flavors and colors, giving you different results. For example, use ube (purple yams), which have vibrant purple flesh, for a deep purple cake. Or use Korean or Japanese sweet potatoes, which have dark purple skins with pale yellow flesh, for a more chestnut-like flavor.

Spicy Salted Caramel Chocolate Bars

Caramel shortbread is a dessert that has too many names: Some people call it millionaire's shortbread, while others call it caramel squares or chocolate caramel shortbread. But, regardless of the name, there's one thing that never changes: layers of buttery shortbread, caramel, and a chocolate layer. These three components create an unforgettable bite.

I wanted to keep the integrity of the dessert but with my twists. So, instead of a traditional shortbread cookie layer, I've swapped it for a graham cracker crust. It still holds its shape but adds a delicious snap. The caramel layer is not your average caramel: It's not only salted but also spiced with chili crisp. These two ingredients give the caramel layer personality and balance the intensely sweet caramel, making it even more satisfying. The final layer of chocolate also has a little bit of chili crisp, but it's subtle because the chocolate flavors are pretty dominant.

Creating the clear contrast of each layer takes a little more time, but it's worth the effort. If you need a mood-boosting, pick-me-up dessert, this is it!

MAKES 9 TO 16 SQUARES

GRAHAM CRACKER CRUST

7 oz [200 g] graham crackers, broken into pieces

½ cup [113 g] unsalted butter

CARAMEL LAYER

1 cup [200 g] dark brown sugar

One 14 oz [400 g] can sweetened condensed milk

½ cup [113 g] unsalted butter

¼ cup [60 ml] maple syrup

2 Tbsp Very Nutty Chili Crisp (page 19)

1½ tsp kosher salt

1 tsp vanilla extract

SPICED CHOCOLATE LAYER

2 cups [360 g] chopped semisweet chocolate

¾ cup [180 ml] heavy cream

2 Tbsp unsalted butter

2 Tbsp Very Nutty Chili Crisp (page 19)

Flaky sea salt, for garnish

1. Line a 9 in [23 cm] square baking pan with parchment paper, letting the the parchment hang over the sides of the pan.

2. **To make the graham cracker crust:** Preheat the oven to 350°F [180°C]. In a food processor, add the graham cracker pieces, and run it until the graham crackers become finely ground crumbs. Transfer them to a large bowl.

3. Melt the butter in the microwave or on the stove top. Pour the melted butter over the graham cracker crumbs and stir to combine. Transfer the graham cracker butter mixture to the prepared baking pan.

Using the clean bottom of a measuring cup, firmly press down the graham crackers so they are tightly packed at the bottom of the baking pan. Bake for 10 minutes, or until the edges of the crust start to turn golden brown. Remove from the oven, let cool to room temperature, and place in the freezer while preparing the caramel layer.

4. **To make the caramel layer:** In a medium saucepan over medium heat, add the brown sugar, condensed milk, butter, and maple syrup. Stir until everything is well combined and bring it to a boil. Once it boils, lower the heat to low and continue to simmer while

occasionally stirring until the mixture turns a rich caramel color and has thickened. This

cont'd.

process should take 10 to 15 minutes. Once it's thickened, turn off the heat. Add the chili crisp, salt, and vanilla and mix to combine.

5. Take the baking pan with the graham cracker layer out of the freezer. Pour the caramel over the graham cracker layer and use a silicone spatula to spread it evenly. Carefully put the baking pan with the caramel layer back in the freezer. Freeze for at least an hour before adding a final layer of chocolate.

6. **To make the spiced chocolate layer:** Put the chocolate chips in a medium bowl. In a small pan over medium-low heat, add the heavy cream and butter and bring it to a simmer. Pour the warm cream mixture over the chocolate in the bowl. Stir until the mixture is smooth. Add the chili crisp to the chocolate mixture and stir to combine.

7. Take out the baking pan from the freezer again. Pour the chocolate layer over the caramel layer in the prepared baking pan. Using a silicone spatula, spread it evenly. Put it in the refrigerator for at least an hour or until the chocolate layer is fully set.

8. Take the shortbread out of the baking pan. Sprinkle the flaky salt on top and slice it into nine or sixteen squares. To make clean slices, warm the knife by running it under hot water for a few seconds. Carefully wipe it dry before slicing. Wipe the knife clean with a clean towel as you go. Serve immediately. The bars can be stored in the refrigerator, preferably in an airtight container, for up to 1 week.

ACKNOWLEDGMENTS

I don't even know where to begin now that I've wrapped up this project! This book wouldn't be possible without the efforts of so many people.

First, thank you to everyone at Chronicle Books for helping me toward one of my life goals. Thank you, Deanne Katz, for finding me and trusting me to make this happen. And a big shout-out to my incredible editor, Dena Rayess, for answering all my questions and ensuring that this book would come together successfully even though I had so much doubt. Big thanks to the whole Chronicle Books team working on this project: Rachel Harrell, Jessica Ling, Mikayla Butchart, Lauren Salkeld, Tera Killip, Steve Kim, Keely Thomas-Menter, and Samantha Simon.

Big thanks to my fantastic agent, Jon Michael Darga. Our connection sparked from the second we spoke on the phone, and I feel so blessed to have you throughout my cookbook journey. Thank you for playing many roles, including unofficial therapist. And thank you to my dear friend and cookbook mentor, Jesse Szewczyk, for advising me from the start.

Big shout-outs to my recipe testers who gave me so much insight, encouragement, and feedback on these spicy recipes: Ashley Noh, Ayako Kaneyoshi, Dami Lee, Dan Ahn, Dawn Weiyi Cai, Diane Paik, Elizabeth Hart, Jieqian Zhang, Justine Lee, Nicole Zhu, Stefani Kung, Trent Pheifer, Umi Syam, and Yuchen Ye. I appreciate each of you so much; this book is so special thanks to your help.

And extra-special shout-outs to two friends who gave me the most feedback and insight throughout my recipe development process: Irene Yoo and Jase Kingsland-Shim. Irene, you've encouraged me more than anyone throughout the process. I'm forever grateful to have you in my life, and thank you for letting me cook so many chili crisp dishes in your kitchen. Jase, without your genius ideas and suggestions, I wouldn't have been able to finish this book. Thank you for always sharing your wisdom and creative takes about life and cooking.

Major thanks to my chili crisp photo team: Heami Lee, Pearl Jones, Gözde Eker, Mieko Takahashi, and Julia Rose. And, special thanks to Jean Lee, who made my visual dream possible by bringing these incredibly talented people into my life. Heami, I can't describe how lucky I feel to have worked on this book with you. It truly means the world; words fall short in expressing my immense respect and love for you.

Thank you to my beautiful family, in both Korea and Alabama, for the endless amount of support. I'm beyond thankful for so much love and support from my Korean mom 엄마, Korean dad 아빠, Princess, Lurch, my Korean brother 장서형, and my Alabama brothers, Paul and Foard. I would be nothing without you guys.

Thank you, Salvatore Franchino, for eating so much chili crisp with me and letting me fill the kitchen with the smell of chili crisp for months.

And, lastly, thanks to all the chili crisp lovers and enthusiasts for helping me take you on this spicy adventure. It's been so fun to share my life story and nerd out with this incredible condiment with you.

INDEX